The Angler's Guide to
Twelve Classic Trout Streams in Michigan

"Waiting for the Hatch," by Edna Whyte

The Angler's Guide to
Twelve Classic Trout Streams in Michigan

Gerth E. Hendrickson

Ann Arbor

THE UNIVERSITY OF MICHIGAN PRESS

NOTE: The information in this book is based on more than twenty years of experience fishing and studying these streams and is accurate and dependable to the best of the author's knowledge. However, no book can anticipate all the problems and hazards a fisherman or boater may encounter on these streams. The author assumes no responsibility for accidents or injury caused by failure to observe all rules of safety.

Copyright © by The University of Michigan 1985, 1994
All rights reserved
Published in the United States of America by
The University of Michigan Press
Manufactured in the United States of America

2000   1999   5   4   3

Library of Congress Cataloging in Publication Data

Hendrickson, G. E. (Gerth Edison), 1916–
    The angler's guide to twelve classic trout streams in Michigan /
Gerth E. Hendrickson.
        p.   cm.
    Rev. ed. of: The angler's guide to ten classic trout streams in
Michigan. c1985.
    Includes bibliographical references and index.
    ISBN 0-472-08272-8 (alk. paper)
    1. Trout fishing—Michigan—Guidebooks.   2. Michigan—Guidebooks.
I. Hendrickson, G. E. (Gerth Edison), 1916–   Angler's guide to ten
classic trout streams in Michigan.   II. Title.   III. Title: Twelve
classic trout streams in Michigan.
SH688.U6H46   1994
799.1'755—dc20   94-26044
                                                                CIP

Front cover photo: James Adams, Adams Photography, Grayling, Michigan

Preface

In streamside conversations with fellow fishermen and fisherwomen in Michigan, Wisconsin, and as far off as California, I have found new friends who are familiar with *The Angler's Guide to Ten Classic Trout Streams in Michigan*. It is gratifying to know that my book has been helpful to my fellow anglers. The addition of two first-class trout streams, the Pine and the Jordan, should be useful to anglers who want to add variety to their fishing opportunities. The Pine is noted for excellent fishing for resident rainbow trout. It is probably the best stream for resident rainbows in Michigan. The Jordan offers some fine fishing for small brookies in the upper reaches and some large lake-run browns and steelhead in the lower river. For anglers who like especially to fish the *Hexagenia* hatch, the Hex hatch on the Jordan lasts longer than on most Michigan rivers, often continuing into early August.

Some changes have occurred in recent years in fish populations, fishing regulations, and camping and access sites on Michigan trout streams. I have tried to include all such changes in this enlarged edition. For information on future changes contact the appropriate regional office of the Michigan Department of Natural Resources and the U.S. Forestry Division at local district offices.

As in the past, I will be happy to hear from any of my readers. I cannot say, as Will Rogers is quoted as saying, that I never met a man I didn't like, but I can say truly that I have never met a trout fisher I didn't like. I wish you all good luck and good fishing.

To my wife

Acknowledgments

In the more than twenty years I have fished and studied these rivers I have obtained information and instruction from many people. Unfortunately, I cannot name all of them, for some are no longer known to me. I am especially grateful to Dr. Gaylord Alexander for helping me in my earlier research on these rivers and providing information on recent changes. Dr. Leonard Allison also helped me in my early studies on the Au Sable and other rivers and made his laboratory available for water analyses. Gerald Myers of Gaylord gave helpful advice and information on the Pigeon, Sturgeon, and Black. Other Michigan Department of Natural Resources people who provided information on recent changes on the rivers include Douglas Carter (Pere Marquette), Lee Mrojinski, Ralph Hay, and Tom Rozich (Pere Marquette, Pine, and Rifle), Steve Swan (Pigeon, Sturgeon, Black, and Jordan), and Andrew Nuhfer (Au Sable system).

Ed Hansen and Bob Stuber of the U.S. Forest Service provided information on the problem of bed load of sand on the Pine and efforts being made to improve the fishery on this river. Charlie Doonan worked with me on earlier studies on most of these rivers and is coauthor of the series of hydrologic atlases published by the U.S. Geological Survey. Dick Brown helped check out some of the access sites on the Pine and Jordan and paddled at the stern on our canoe reconnaissance of these streams.

The local librarians in Grayling, Gaylord, Roscommon, Rose City, Baldwin, and Traverse City provided clues to sources of historical information on several of the rivers. Special thanks for furnishing historical materials go to Barbara Sanback of Rose City (Rifle), Martin Melkild of Traverse City (Boardman), George Dechow of Baldwin (Pere Marquette), and Margaret Jenson of Grayling (South Branch of the Au Sable).

Finally, I am indebted to Horace Failing and Dick Bittner of Grayling and many other angler companions who shared their knowledge and skill on these rivers over the years.

Contents

What This Book Is About   1

What Makes a Stream Fit for Trout—
   How to Keep It That Way   15

How to Use This Guide   23

Michigan's Au Sable River   24

South Branch of the Au Sable   52

North Branch of the Au Sable   76

Manistee River   94

Pigeon River   118

Sturgeon River   142

Black River   170

Boardman River   192

Rifle River   208

Pere Marquette River   224

Pine River   246

Jordan River   270

References Cited   291

Other Sources of Information   293

Index   295

Figures

Au Sable River

1. Location map of the Upper Au Sable River   28
2. Site No. 1. Au Sable River Canoe State Forest Campground   32
3. Site No. 2. Burton's Landing State Forest Campground   34
4. Site No. 3. Louie's Landing Road   36
5. Site No. 4. Keystone Landing State Forest Campground   38
6. Site No. 5. Thendara Road   40
7. Site No. 6. Stephan Bridge Public Access Site   42
8. Site No. 7. Wakeley Bridge Public Access Site   44
9. Site No. 8. White Pine Canoe State Forest Campground   46
10. Site No. 9. Conners Flat Public Access Site   48
11. Site No. 10. Rainbow Bend State Forest Campground   50

South Branch of the Au Sable

12. Location map of the South Branch Au Sable   56
13. Road access to sites in the Mason Tract   57
14. Site No. 1. Chase Bridge Public Access Site   62
15. Site No. 2. Leline Road   64
16. Site No. 3. The Castle Public Access Site   66
17. Site No. 4. Downey's Public Access Site   68
18. Site No. 5. Dogtown Public Access Site   70

19. Site No. 6. Canoe Harbor State Forest Campground   72
20. Site No. 7. Smith Bridge Public Access Site   74

North Branch of the Au Sable
21. Location map of the North Branch Au Sable   80
22. Site No. 1. Pipe Springs Public Access Site   82
23. Site No. 2. Sheep Ranch Public Access Site   84
24. Site No. 3. Twin Bridge   86
25. Site No. 4. Lovells Bridge   88
26. Site No. 5. Lower Public Access Site   90
27. Site No. 6. Kelloggs Bridge   92

Manistee River
28. Location map of the Manistee, Deward to M-72   98
29. Location map of the Manistee, M-72 to Sharon   99
30. Site No. 1. Deward   102
31. Site No. 2. Cameron Bridge   104
32. Site No. 3. Red Bridge   106
33. Site No. 4. Upper Manistee River State Forest
    Campground   108
34. Site No. 5. Manistee River Bridge State Forest
    Campground   110
35. Site No. 6. CCC Bridge State Forest Campground   112
36. Site No. 7. Sandy Bottom Public Access Site   114
37. Site No. 8. North Sharon Road Bridge   116

Pigeon River
38. Location map of the Pigeon River   122
39. Site No. 1. County Parking Lot   126
40. Site No. 2. Old Vanderbilt Road Bridge   128
41. Site No. 3. Pigeon Bridge State Forest
    Campground   130
42. Site No. 4. Pigeon River State Forest Campground   132
43. Site No. 5. County Line Road   134
44. Site No. 6. Tin Bridge Public Access Site   136

45. Site No. 7. Pine Grove State Forest Campground   138

46. Site No. 8. Red Bridge   140

Sturgeon River

47. Location map of the Sturgeon, Poquette Road Bridge to Green Timbers Public Access Site   146

48. Location map of the Sturgeon, Trowbridge Road Public Access Site to White Road Bridge   147

49. Site No. 1. Poquette Road Bridge   150

50. Site No. 2. Doc Sehls Bridge   152

51. Site No. 3. Old Vanderbilt Road Bridge   154

52. Site No. 4. Sturgeon Bridge   156

53. Site No. 5. Green Timbers Public Access Site   158

54. Site No. 6. Trowbridge Road Public Access Site   160

55. Site No. 7. Scott Road Public Access Site   162

56. Site No. 8. Haakwood State Forest Campground   164

57. Site No. 9. Rondo Road Bridge Public Access Site   166

58. Site No. 10. White Road Bridge   168

Black River

59. Location map of the Black, headwaters to Black River Ranch   174

60. Location map of the Black, Black River Ranch to Tower Pond   175

61. Site No. 1. McKinnon Bend Public Access Site   178

62. Site No. 2. Tin Shanty Bridge   180

63. Site No. 3. South Tower Public Access Site   182

64. Site No. 4. Main River Bridge   184

65. Site No. 5. Clark Bridge   186

66. Site No. 6. Crocket Bridge   188

67. Site No. 7. Wigglesworth Road Public Easement   190

Boardman River

68. Location map of the Upper Boardman   196

69. Site No. 1. North Branch Bridge   198

70. Site No. 2. South Branch Bridge   200
71. Site No. 3. Forks State Forest Campground   202
72. Site No. 4. Brown Bridge Road Public Access Site   204
73. Site No. 5. Scheck's Place State Forest
     Campground   206

Rifle River

74. Location map of the Rifle   212
75. Site No. 1. Rifle River Recreation Area   214
76. Site No. 2. Sage Lake Road   216
77. Site No. 3. Rifle River State Forest Campground   218
78. Site No. 4. Peters Road   220
79. Site No. 5. Selkirk Bridge   222

Pere Marquette River

80. Location map of the Pere Marquette, headwaters to
     Bowman Bridge Public Access Site   228
81. Location map of the Pere Marquette, Bowman Bridge
     Public Access Site to Walhalla Public Access Site   229
82. Site No. 1. The Forks south of Baldwin Public Access
     Site   232
83. Site No. 2. M-37 Bridge south of Baldwin Public Access
     Site   234
84. Site No. 3. Gleason's Landing   236
85. Site No. 4. Bowman Bridge Public Access Site   238
86. Site No. 5. Sulak Public Access Site   240
87. Site No. 6. Upper Branch Bridge Public Access
     Site   242
88. Site No. 7. Walhalla Bridge Public Access Site   244

Pine River

89. Location map of the Pine River, Silver Creek State Forest
     Campground to Peterson Bridge Campground   252
90. Location map of the Pine River, Edgetts Bridge to public
     access sites   253
91. Site No. 1. Edgetts Bridge Public Access Site   256

92. Site Nos. 2 and 3. Public access sites near Skookum Bridge   258
93. Site No. 4. Silver Creek State Forest Campground   260
94. Site No. 5. Lincoln Bridge State Forest Campground   262
95. Site No. 6. Elm Flats Canoe Landing   264
96. Site No. 7. Dobson Bridge Canoe Landing   266
97. Site No. 8. Peterson Bridge National Forest Campground   268

Jordan River

98. Location map of the Jordan River, headwaters to East Jordan   274
99. Site No. 1. Old Bridge Public Access Site   276
100. Site No. 2. Pinney Bridge Public Access Site   278
101. Site No. 3. Graves Crossing State Forest Campground   280
102. Site No. 4. Chestonia Bridge Public Access Site   282
103. Site No. 5. Webster Bridge Public Access Site   284
104. Site No. 6. Electric Weir Public Access Site   286
105. Site No. 7. Rogers Road Bridge Public Access Site   288

What This Book Is About

This book was written to tell you, a trout fisherman, what you need to know to get the most enjoyment possible from fishing some of the best trout streams east of the Rockies. Each of these streams has a large population of stream-bred trout, ample public access, and water favorable to the wading fisherman. All are large enough and productive enough to accommodate much fishing pressure, yet all have waters where you have a good chance to fish alone. As an added attraction, these are streams of great natural beauty that provide aesthetic pleasure as well as the opportunity to catch trout.

The term "fisherman," as used here, is intended to include all anglers for trout, both men and women. Although relatively few in number, the women who come to fish these streams are as skillful and as dedicated to the sport as any man.

When you plan to fish a stream you want to know how wide it is and how deep. Is it wide enough for fly casting or so narrow that it is easier to use a spinning rod or bait? Is it shallow enough for easy wading or so deep it will overtop your waders? What are the bottom materials like? Will you stand on firm sand or gravel, slip on hard clay or muddy stones, or sink into soft sand or mud? How about the velocity of flow? Is it slow enough that you can wade easily upstream or so fast that you will be swept off your feet? All of these things are described or shown on the maps.

The northern part of Michigan's Lower Peninsula has more top-quality trout streams than any other comparable area east of the Rocky Mountains. The streams described here are classic in that each is "an excellent model of its kind" and "famous as traditional or typical." Much of the lore of trout fishing originated on these streams. I have tried to include streams that will appeal to all kinds of trout fishermen. Most of the streams are narrow and brushy in the headwaters, favoring the bait and spin fishermen. All have wadable waters broad enough for easy fly casting. Wading varies from relatively easy in the "Holy Water" of the Au Sable to difficult or impossible in much of the Pine. Most have reaches suitable for boat fishing. Five of the streams have reaches with special rules limiting lures to flies only. Several of the streams have excellent runs of steelhead and lake-run browns in their lower reaches, but this guide is chiefly concerned with the resident trout fishery.

These are young streams in geologic terms, having settled down in their present courses after the retreat of the glaciers some twelve to thirteen thousand years ago. With the retreat of the ice the earliest Indians moved into the area and used the rivers as a source of food and drink and as highways for canoe travel. The early white traders used the rivers for the same purpose and left the streams and woods much as they had found them.

With the coming of the lumbermen in the mid-1800s all of this changed. The riverbanks were stripped of their timber, and log drives worked havoc on the riverbeds, degrading their capacity for food production and spawning for the fish. Nevertheless, the fishing, first for grayling and then for trout, was very good, according to old-time residents of the area. Following the lumber boom, some attempts were made to farm parts of the land, but the sandy soils and short growing season soon discouraged most farmers.

During the 1930s, much of the land became tax-delinquent property and reverted to state ownership. With good management, the forest cover has been renewed over most of these lands. Today, crystal clear trout streams flow through some of the most attractive forests of the Midwest.

Bait, Lure, and Fly

Like most fishermen, I caught my first trout on a worm, and I have fished many a trout stream with worms since then. I now fish for trout with flies, not because I consider it more sporting, but because it is more fun. I have not tried fishing for trout with spinning tackle, but I have seen some fine trout caught with this equipment, and the spin fishermen seem to enjoy their sport as much as the fly-fishermen.

I am glad to have some parts of trout streams restricted to fly-fishing, but would not like to see all trout waters designated flies-only. The bait and spin fishermen have as much right to their sport as the fly-fishermen, and all have a common cause. It is the trout that bring them to the streams, and all want to preserve the trout streams and the trout fishery. The method of fishing should not be allowed to alienate one group from the others.

Brooks, Browns, Rainbows, and Grayling

The only trout native to Michigan streams was the brookie, and even the brook trout was not originally found in most of the streams of the Lower Peninsula. It seems fairly well established that there were brook trout in the streams of the Upper Peninsula when white men first explored these waters, but only a few of the northernmost streams of the Lower Peninsula had trout at that time. Walter J. Hunsaker, president of the Michigan Fish Commission, wrote in 1919 (Mershon 1923, pp. 147–48): "Except for the coast region from Traverse City on the Lake Michigan side to Rogers City on the Lake Huron side, practically all the brook trout that have inhabitated the Lower Peninsula waters were artificially bred and artificially planted."

In a letter to William B. Mershon (Mershon 1923, pp. 152–53), Mr. Seymour Bower, superintendent of fisheries in Michigan, said:

> As to the southern limit of native trout streams in Michigan, I think it is very well established that native trout had worked down as far south as the Boardman and its tributaries but no farther; and they inhabited most if not all of the streams flowing into Lake Michigan between the Boardman and the Straits. . . . Regarding the Lake Huron streams south of the straits, I think Bissel is not so certain as to how far down the trout had worked, but believe he concluded that Hammonds Bay or not far below was the dividing line.

From these accounts it appears that, of the streams described here, only the Pigeon, Sturgeon, Black, Jordan, and Boardman had native trout before any plantings. The remaining streams were the home of the grayling and had no trout until planted by man in the late 1800s.

The first hatching and raising of brook trout in Michigan reportedly was by N. W. Clark of Clarkson, Michigan in 1867 (Mershon 1923, pp. 153–54), and the first planting of brook trout was by A. N. Mershon, the father of William B. Mershon. The brookies were planted in the Tobacco River in 1870. By 1874, brook trout were being planted in several streams, including the Pere Marquette, the Little Manistee, and the Manistee rivers.

The first record of planting rainbow trout in Michigan was in the mid-1870s, when Mr. Clark with Daniel Fitzhugh of Bay City made a small planting of rainbows in the Au Sable. The first planting of rainbows by the Michigan Fish Commission was in the Paw Paw River in Van Buren County and the Boyne River in Charlevoix County in 1880. Most of the rainbows now caught in Michigan streams are lake-run trout or steelhead. There is evidence that the steelhead compete with the resident trout, and some of the streams that have heavy steelhead runs no longer support a first-class resident fishery. Fishermen report that the fishing for resident browns on the Pere Marquette and the Rifle has declined in recent years, and the resident fishery on the Little Manistee has essentially disappeared. The Pacific salmon also compete with the resident trout on some of these streams, but salmon are barred from the Little Manistee.

On April 14, 1984, the West Michigan Chapter of Trout Unlimited celebrated the hundredth anniversary of the first planting of browns in the Pere Marquette River system. The first hatching of browns by the Michigan Fish Commission were put in the state's waters in 1889 (Mershon 1923, p. 152). The browns grew and thrived and are now the most abundant resident trout in most of the Lower Peninsula trout streams.

There seems to be little doubt that grayling and brook trout existed together in some Michigan streams before any trout were planted by man. If this is so, then the trout cannot be blamed entirely for the demise of the grayling. Stories of old-time residents suggest that the grayling was less wary of man and more easily caught than even the brook trout. An easy prey of the fisherman and less tolerant than the trout of degradation of the stream itself, the Michigan grayling appears to have been a victim of man's mishandling of his environment. Mershon (1923, p. 168) paraphrasing a great writer, said: "Doubtless God could make a better fish than the Michigan grayling, but doubtless, He never did."

In recent years, grayling have been planted in several lakes and streams in Michigan, including the Au Sable below Mio dam and in the Manistee below the M-72 bridge. The success of these plantings has not yet been determined. However, Gaylord Alexander (personal communication, 1987) believes the environmental quality of the lakes and streams is adequate for the grayling to survive. Because the grayling are so easily caught, catch-and-release regulations will probably be necessary for several years. It will be a great victory for fisheries management if grayling can once again be caught in Michigan streams.

A Word about Safe Wading

For each of the access sites described in this book I have provided information on wading conditions. These are the conditions you may expect during the regular trout season at normal late-spring and summer flows. In early spring, when the rivers are high, and after heavy rains in any season, the streams flow deeper and swifter, and wading conditions are quite different—more difficult and more dangerous. Wading conditions also change in places from year to year. The shallow water you waded easily last year may be scoured so deep that it overtops your waders. Or the deep hole you had to avoid may be filled with sand. A thin veneer of gravel may be washed away, exposing the underlying slippery clay. Be especially watchful for such changes on your first trip of the season.

The twelve streams included in this book, like all first-class trout streams in the Midwest, have a large component of groundwater flow, and consequently are relatively steady in discharge. Nevertheless, all streams fluctuate to some degree. The Pere Marquette, for example, has an average annual range in stage at Scottville of about 3.5 feet. The Manistee near Grayling rises only about 12 inches in an average year, but a rise of even 6 inches can change wading conditions drastically.

When you are about to wade into an unfamiliar stream you should consider the four factors that chiefly influence safe wading, namely, depth of water, velocity of flow, character of streambed, and underwater snags and other hazards. I am assuming, first of all, that you are in good physical condition.

Obviously you don't want to go into water that will overtop your waders, but the depth, coupled with the velocity, can also determine whether you can stand up in the stream. As a rule of thumb, you should not try to wade a stream if the depth in feet, multiplied by the velocity of flow in feet per second, is greater than ten. I do not suggest that you try to get an accurate measure of the velocity of flow before you enter the stream, but if the flow appears swift and the depth is greater than about 2 feet you had better not try it. Also, if you are having difficulty wading where the water is 2 feet deep, you will almost surely be swept off your feet if you step into water 3 feet deep.

The rule of ten cited above assumes a firm bed of sand or gravel and a strong fisherman. If the streambed is slippery clay or greasy rocks the depth-times-velocity factor for safe wading is substantially smaller. Soft sand and mud also make wading difficult and sometimes dangerous. Soft sand is especially treacherous when approaching a deep hole from the upstream side. If you get too close the sand will give way beneath your feet, you will not be able to back out, and you will get a ducking.

Most Lower Peninsula streams are bottomed in sand and gravel, but there are areas of boulders and patches of hard slippery clay, as well as soft sand and mud. A few of the streams have small areas of bedrock or hard clay or marl resembling bedrock. The bedrock and hard clay can cause problems to the wading fisherman because he may step from knee-deep water on the hard bottom to a hole over his head in the unconsolidated sand and gravel. The patches of clay are especially troublesome because they are often light in color and can be mistaken for sand. Felt soles are not much help on this clay.

Underwater snags and trash of all kinds can be hazardous to the wading fisherman, especially at night. One way to avoid these hazards is to probe ahead with a wading staff. If you don't like to carry a staff you may be able to detect some of the hazards by probing ahead with one foot while keeping the other firmly planted on the bottom.

Wading at night is always difficult. The underwater snags, logjams, and boulders that are easily avoided in daylight may trip you up or rip your waders at night. The deep holes that overtop your waders are hard to see. If you like to be on the stream after dark, it is, no doubt, safer to fish with a companion than to go it alone. Nevertheless, I usually prefer to fish alone at night. I enjoy the solitude and try to compensate for any increased danger by taking greater care to wade safely.

It is almost always safer to wade upstream than down. It is easier to back away from danger with the current helping you than when the flow is pushing you into trouble. When wading an unfamiliar stream be especially watchful for a narrowing of the channel. This always means more difficult wading, for the narrowing channel means deeper water or faster flow, or both.

Another danger to the wading fisherman is a logjam or snag approached from the upstream side. A swift current may pin you against the log and you may not be able to back away. If a logjam or snag blocks your way it is safer to go around it than to try to climb over it or duck under it.

Avoid wading under bridges. The headwalls usually confine the stream to a narrow channel with consequent increase in depth and velocity. Also, you will almost always run into large boulders, broken concrete, or underwater pilings to trip you up. Be on the lookout for a deep pool that commonly forms just below the bridge.

If you think, perhaps, that I dwell too much on the dangers that go with wading a trout stream, I can only say that I have experienced, or narrowly avoided, most of the disasters that can occur to the careless wader. Having eyes only for a rising trout on the South Branch of the Au Sable, I tripped over a large boulder, fell headfirst, and broke a prized fly rod. I was swept off my feet trying to wade water too fast and deep on the Sturgeon, and was pinned against a logjam on the Pigeon. Although warned of the danger, I had to swim for it in the Whirlpool on the Au Sable mainstream. In a small spring-fed creek in southwestern Wisconsin I sank up to my hips in quicksand. I managed to pull myself out, but my boots are still buried in the creek. Trout fishing is too much fun to allow it to be spoiled by avoidable wading accidents.

Camping

Each of the rivers described here has campgrounds or access sites where camping is permitted. Accommodations range from undeveloped access sites with no facilities whatever to campgrounds with running water, showers, and flush toilets. Some public access sites are posted against camping. Camping is permitted anywhere on state forest lands except where specifically prohibited or where a developed campground is available within 1 mile. Prospective campers on undeveloped sites should obtain a Camp Registration Card (Form PR 1313) from any Michigan Department of Natural Resources (DNR) field office. Registration cards can also be obtained by mail addressed to the State Forest Operations Section, P.O. Box 30028, Lansing, MI 48909.

The most numerous campgrounds on the rivers are the Michigan state forest campgrounds. These are generally equipped with hand pumps, toilets, picnic tables, and fireplaces. Registration is on-site with no advance reservations accepted. U.S. Forest Service campgrounds on the Pine and Pere Marquette rivers are similarly equipped, although some are a bit more elaborate. Primitive camping is also allowed anywhere in the Huron-Manistee National Forests except within 200 feet of water. Campers in undeveloped camps are required to leave the campsites clean and uncluttered, exactly as they find them.

Some of the Michigan state forest campgrounds on the twelve streams included here may be closed, temporarily or permanently. All such closures reported to date are noted in the site descriptions. Information on future closures can be obtained from the Michigan Department of Natural Resources, (517) 335-3338.

Although the number of state forest campgrounds and the number of sites per campground have been reduced in recent years, Mr. Dean Sandell, recreation program leader, reports that the usage in camper days per camp is greater. The security in the campgrounds is generally quite good, probably owing in part to the Host Volunteer Program. Volunteers live in the camp during the camping season without charge. In return for this privilege, they are available to assist and advise the campers and generally see to it that the camp runs smoothly.

None of the campgrounds at Michigan state parks are directly on the rivers described here, but some are close enough to provide good access to the rivers. Facilities at these parks are more elaborate than at the state forest parks or the national forest parks. Some offer rustic cabins at a modest fee.

Boating Safety

Boat fishing is popular on the unwadable reaches of some of these streams. The wadable reaches also are sometimes fished by boat in order to cover more water in an evening's fishing or to fish the inaccessible areas. Anglers no longer able to wade the streams can add years to their fishing by taking to guided boats.

Most of the streams described here have reaches that can be safely floated at normal flows by boaters of moderate competence. A few, like the Pere Marquette and Pine, require greater skill, and one, the Sturgeon, should be attempted by experts only. The reaches best suited to boat fishing are those having slow to moderate velocity and wide and open enough to allow plenty of casting room. Swift and narrow reaches with overhanging trees and branches, called "sweepers," are difficult and sometimes dangerous for all boaters, whether fishing or not. The sweepers should be carefully avoided at all times as they can cause an upset on even the most placid of streams. Note the set of the current ahead of you and position your boat upstream to allow a wide margin of safety.

Streams that are easily traveled at normal flows can become hazardous even to experienced boaters at high water. The greater depth may make it easier to get over some of the rocks and shoals, but the increased velocity can sweep you into snags and branches that will overturn your boat. Some years ago two young boaters narrowly escaped drowning trying to float the Pigeon River at high water. Their boat capsized against a tree, but fortunately they were pulled to safety by a streamgager who had seen their plight.

None of the stream segments described here have rapids that would pose much of a challenge to an expert boater, but the amateur may damage his canoe or small boat on the rocks in places on the Pere Marquette and the Black. In *Michigan Canoe Trails* the novice is advised to portage around Rainbow Rapids on the Pere Marquette. Logjams that block the entire channel are another source of danger. It often appears easier to lift the boat over the jam than to portage around it, but portaging is usually the safer way to go.

There is sometimes a great temptation to try to boat water that is beyond your competence. Some contend that this is a way to improve your boating skills, but you will have little opportunity to use these skills if you drown. The best way to learn boating skills is to float the streams with an experienced guide who can protect you from disaster while you are learning how it's done.

On Not Getting Lost

Because most of the better trout streams are located in sparsely settled areas, special precautions should be taken to avoid getting lost. It is surprisingly easy to get lost on a trout stream. One cold September morning on the Escanaba River near Gwinn I managed to do it in just about five minutes. I was walking down the left bank looking for a good place to enter the river. When I came to a large downed pine blocking my path it was easier to go around it on the landward side than to enter the river there, so I veered off to my left. When I rounded the pine I angled off to my right again, thinking to come back to the riverbank a few hundred feet down-stream. But I walked and I walked—one hundred yards, two hundred yards, a quarter-mile—and the river was not yet in sight. I reached in my pocket for the compass I always carry. I had left it in my other jacket. Dark clouds had blotted out the sun. The wind was blowing from the north, or was it the west? I knew the river had to be to the west, but which way was west? Resisting the impulse to run, I forced myself to sit down with my back against a tree and think things over. In a few minutes the clouds were blown away and the sun came out again. With the sun at my back I walked rapidly, very rapidly, westward and soon saw the welcome gleam of the river ahead of me.

It is always a good idea to carry a compass, even when fishing a familiar stream. Carry it in your fishing vest or jacket, and, if you change jackets, be sure to transfer the compass, too. The compass is a big help, but it may not always be enough. You should also carry the best map of the area you can get. A U.S. Geological Survey topographic map usually is the best. These can be purchased from the DNR in Lansing. Before you leave your car, mark your location on the map and pencil an arrow showing the direction you plan to go to the river. Even if you think you know the country very well you may find the map reassuring.

Carry also a good flashlight with fresh batteries, a supply of matches in a waterproof container, and a sandwich, candy bar, or other concentrated food. If you do get lost these things can add much to your comfort and peace of mind.

When fishing an unfamiliar stream in a wilderness area it is a good idea to mark the spot where you enter the stream. Tie a white handkerchief or other marker to a bush overhanging the stream.

When you are ready to leave the stream you will know just where to get out. Be sure to take your marker with you when you leave.

If you fish alone you should let someone know where you are going and when you will be coming back. Then, if you do get lost, you will know that help will soon be on the way.

Rules, Regulations, and Fish You Should Not Eat

In the site descriptions and elsewhere in this book I have referred to "flies-only" and "special regulation" water in some reaches of the streams. You should understand that these rules and regulations change from year to year, and you should be aware of those currently in force. When you purchase your fishing license and trout stamp you will be provided with the latest issue of *Michigan Fishing Guide*, which summarizes the rules and regulations on Michigan fishing.

This guide also contains a *Public Health Advisory* that cautions you against eating certain fish in some waters and *all* fish in other waters. Fortunately, none of the rivers described here are currently included in these lists. However, migratory trout and salmon and other fish that enter these rivers from contaminated sources *are* included in this advisory. These lists can change with time also, so be sure you check the latest guide.

Trout fishermen generally have the reputation of being good citizens on the streams, and usually comply with both the spirit and letter of the rules. Many anglers now return most or all of their catch to the water. Limiting the kill of trout is helpful, but the future of trout fishing also requires the preservation of favorable trout habitat. You can help preserve the trout streams by supporting conservation organizations such as Trout Unlimited and the Federation of Fly Fishermen. Other steps you can take to maintain the trout fishery are described in the section "What Makes a Stream Fit for Trout—How to Keep It That Way."

Trout Stream Maps

For each of the streams I have included a set of maps. The small-scale location maps are based on county highway maps and show the channel of the stream and the major public roads leading to the stream. Numbered access sites are also shown on the location maps.

For each of the rivers, five to ten access sites open to the public are mapped at a larger scale. I have not tried to cover every possible access, but have included enough to give you several weeks of excellent fishing on each of these classic streams. The larger-scale site maps show the river channel in greater detail. These are chiefly based on topographic maps and show most of the roads and trails at the time the map was made. Not all roads shown are open to the public. Some newer roads and trails, especially those related to recent oil and gas development, are not shown. Remember that the condition of the roads also can change. The road you drove with ease may be blocked by deep potholes or downed timber the next time you try it. The width of the stream on the site maps is exaggerated in order to show the character of the bottom materials. The maps show only the predominate materials. An occasional boulder or small areas of bedrock, cemented sands, hard slippery clay, or soft sand and mud may occur at almost any site. The maps and text together should tell you what you need to know about the fishing conditions at each site.

Michigan Flies and Fly Hatches

Michigan has some of the best flytiers in America, and several important flies originated here. Probably the most famous Michigan fly is the Adams, designed by Len Halladay of Mayfield, Michigan, and named for his friend, C. F. Adams, of Lorain, Ohio. This fly was first fished on the Boardman River near Mayfield, but is now used by fishermen throughout the United States. Other effective flies originating in Michigan include the Michigan Caddis, the Michigan Hopper, the Borcher's, the Skunk, and Robert's Yellow Drake. The Borcher's is similar to the Adams, but has a dark brown body. The Skunk, tied wet or dry, is mostly black and white with white rubber legs. The wet Skunk usually is weighted and is hard to cast, but it can be very effective. Some of these flies are little known outside of Michigan, but they probably would take trout on most Midwestern and Eastern trout streams.

An excellent description of Michigan flies and fly hatches appeared in the May/June, 1983, issue of *Michigan Sportsman* magazine. The author, Mr. Kenneth L. Peterson of the *Flint Journal,* and Mr. Tom Petrie, publisher of the *Michigan Sportsman,* have given me permission to reproduce some of this information here.

Of course there are other fly hatches that appear on Michigan streams, but the fisherman who carries these patterns will be prepared for most of the action. Every fisherman has a few favorites. My fly box always has a supply of Adams in sizes 12 to 16, and I use these whenever I am not sure what fly the fish are taking. Most fly-fishermen also carry a supply of wet flies, nymphs, and streamers, although they may seldom use them when any surface activity is apparent. The Muddler Minnow, Maribou Muddler in various colors, Matuka streamers, and wet and dry skunks are popular on most Michigan trout streams.

You should remember that the dates of emergence are approximate only, and can vary substantially with weather conditions. Also, some streams are colder than others, and hatches come later. Whenever possible, you should check with the local anglers to get the best information on the current hatches. You will find them in sporting goods stores, fly shops, bars, barbershops, and coffee shops. Trout fishermen are a friendly people who will gladly share their information with you.

Michigan Flies, Emergence Dates, and Matching Artificial Flies and Size

Insect	Emergence Date	Matching Fly and Size
Ephemerella subvaria	April 25–June 16	Hendrickson, 12–14
Ephemerella invaria	May 3–July 20	Red Quill, 12–14
Ephemerella dorothea	May 12–July 3	Sulpher Dun, 14–16
Ephemera simulans	June 2–July 14	Brown Drake, 8–10
Siphlonurus rapidus	May 26–June 19	Grey Drake, 8–10
alternatus	June 17–July 26	
quebecenis	May 22–June 26	
Hexagenia limbata	June 25–July 10	Michigan Caddis, 4–6
Tricorythodes	July 26–Sept. 7	Black Midge, 20–24
Leptophlebia cupida	May 15–Aug. 31	Black Quill, 12–14
Paraleptophlebia adoptiva	May 4–July 8	Blue-winged Dun, 16–18
Ephemerella lata	June 25–Aug. 13	Blue-winged Olive Dun, 18–20
Brachycentrus numerosis	May 7–June 15	Grannom, 14
lateralis	May 1–June 7	
Hydropsyche slossonae	May 15–Aug. 30	Brown Caddis, 14–16
sparna	May 7–Sept. 15	
Chimarra	May 1–Sept. 7	Black Caddis, 16–18

Source: Kenneth L. Peterson, "Match the Michigan Hatches." *Michigan Sportsman,* May/June, 1983, p. 46.
Mayfly emergence data credit: Leonard and Leonard 1962.
Caddis emergence data credit: Leonard and Leonard 1949.

What Makes a Stream Fit for Trout—How to Keep It That Way

The thick deposits of permeable sand and gravel left by the Pleistocene glaciers are the key to the many outstanding trout streams in the northern part of Michigan's Lower Peninsula. These deposits absorb large quantities of rain and melting snow and feed them gradually to the streams to keep them flowing strong and cool during summer droughts. The water dissolves calcium and magnesium carbonate as it flows through the glacial materials and becomes hard and moderately alkaline—qualities favorable to trout habitat. Because the water entering the streams is cool it absorbs enough oxygen to satisfy the trout's requirements. The glacial deposits also supply the consolidated gravels on the streambed essential to spawning trout.

Under natural conditions these streams are nearly ideal trout waters, but most works of man, unless carefully controlled, will cause some deterioration in trout habitat.

What to Do about Pollution

Probably the greatest potential threat to Michigan trout streams is the discharge of industrial and municipal pollutants into the streams. The DNR has warned against eating certain fish in some of Michigan's lakes and streams because of chemical contaminants. The affected waters are listed in a *Public Health Advisory* included with the *Michigan Fishing Guide* available to all who purchase a Michigan fishing license. None of the streams described here are included in these lists at present, but this is no guarantee of future immunity. Furthermore, the advisory *does* apply to migratory fish that may enter some of these streams. For example, migratory trout and salmon that enter the Pere Marquette from Lake Michigan are included in the warning. The edibility of trout is not of major importance to those fishermen who return most or all of their catch to the water, but who wants to fish in a stream so polluted that the fish are not fit to eat?

The Water Quality Surveillance Section of the Michigan Water Resources Commission monitors the quality of water in Michigan streams. In addition to sampling for chemical analysis, aquatic biologists check the streams for evidence of biologic degradation. These professionals cannot be everywhere at once, however, and the alert fisherman can help by reporting any signs of pollution in his favorite stream. An unusually rank growth of aquatic vegetation suggests an upstream source of nutrient discharge—possibly sewage wastes. Brown or grey slime on the riverbed is even stronger evidence of sewage pollution. Oil slicks on the water, detergent foam, unusual color, and chemical odor are other indicators of contamination. If you suspect that warm water is being discharged into the stream, check the water temperature above and below the point of discharge.

Report any signs of pollution to the Pollution Emergency Alerting System of the DNR. The toll-free number to call is 1-800-292-4706.

Acid Rain

The effect of "acid rain" on the quality of water in lakes and streams has been the subject of increasing concern, especially in the northeastern states and adjacent areas of Canada. Merna and Alexander (1983) studied the effect of snowmelt and early season runoff on the pH and alkalinity of northern Michigan streams. They found a substantial reduction in pH (increased acidity) in some of the flashy streams of the Upper Peninsula. Part of this increased acidity was attributed to the flushing out of natural organic acids from the wetlands, but some of it probably comes from the release of inorganic acids derived from the atmosphere (acid rain). The pH values of Lower Peninsula streams were reduced only slightly because the large groundwater inflow to these streams keeps the water highly buffered.

The reduction of pH in some of Michigan's Upper Peninsula streams may be great enough to reduce the survival of trout fry. Further studies by the DNR will determine if increased acidity from atmospheric sources is becoming a serious threat to Michigan streams.

Sewage Disposal

Sewage effluent entering a trout stream has far-reaching effects beyond the obvious problems of odor and bacterial contamination. The BOD (biochemical oxygen demand) of the wastewater reduces the dissolved oxygen content of the stream. If the amount of wastewater is large in relation to the flow of the stream the dissolved oxygen can go so low as to make the water unfit for trout. The rank growth of aquatic vegetation resulting from the nutrients in the sewage wastes causes a wide fluctuation in the dissolved oxygen content of the stream, ranging from supersaturation in the daytime to well below saturation at night. This effect can extend downstream much farther than the initial decline in dissolved oxygen caused by the BOD of the effluent.

In recent years several communities have substituted sewage lagoons as a means of disposing of municipal wastes instead of discharging sewage effluent directly into trout streams. The town of Grayling, for example, went to sewage lagoon disposal in 1971, as did Roscommon in 1974. Before the change, the sewage effluent from Grayling caused a decline in the nighttime dissolved oxygen content of the Au Sable that extended several miles downstream. The effluent also caused a marked increase in coliform (sewage) bacteria below the outfall, and the nutrients stimulated an extremely dense growth of aquatic vegetation. The effect of the sewage effluent from Roscommon on the South Branch was not as great, probably because the amount of effluent from the smaller town was less.

There is little doubt that the aesthetic quality of the streams is improved since the direct discharge of effluent stopped. The grey-brown slimes are gone and the odor is gone, and the aquatic vegetation is not so rank. But it now appears that the trout population also has declined and the growth rate of the trout is slower (Merron 1982). This is not surprising and was anticipated by some fishery biologists, because many studies have shown that trout populations can be increased by nutrient enrichment of the stream.

Some may now argue that it was a mistake to change to the sewage lagoons, that it would be better to discharge the effluent directly into the river to maintain the larger trout populations that formerly were here. But I don't think so. I, for one, would rather catch fewer and smaller trout in a clean, unpolluted stream than to catch more and larger trout fattened by sewage effluent. Also, I would rather release all my catch, rather than occasionally keeping one or two as I now do, if that would help. Furthermore, how can we know that discharge of sewage effluent will help the trout populations in the long run? As cities grow and sewage wastes increase, nutrient enrichment may become excessive, oxygen content may decline, and the river could eventually become unfit for any trout.

Maintaining the Flow of the Streams

Because the favorable qualities of Michigan trout streams are largely dependent on groundwater inflow to the streams, any activity that reduces this flow is a threat to trout habitat. Drastic changes in land use in the watershed could reduce the amount of water percolating down to the water-bearing formations and consequently the groundwater inflow to the streams. The changes now going on, the construction of streets and roads and parking lots, may cause undesirable amounts of sediment to enter the streams, but they are not great enough to significantly reduce recharge to water-bearing formations. Pumping of high-capacity wells near the rivers can reduce the flow of groundwater to the streams, but the effect on Michigan trout streams probably is minor at present. However, a substantial increase in such pumping could significantly reduce the flow and warm the stream. If a large increase is needed these withdrawals should be managed to minimize the effect on the flow of the stream. Effective management involves location and spacing of wells, regulations on the depth of the producing formations, and control of pumping. This is the work of professionals, but the trout fisherman can insist that management is planned and regulations enforced.

The diversion of water for agricultural use could become a problem in future years. Such diversions could effect the flow of streams if the water is taken directly from the streams or from large-capacity wells near the streams.

What to Do about Impoundments

The effect of impoundments on trout streams is complex and cannot be predicted unless the hydrologic setting is studied. However, because the potential damage is great, trout fishermen should insist that no *new* impoundments are built without such a study. Impoundments inevitably destroy that part of the stream that is flooded and may cause undesirable changes in streamflow, water temperature, and bottom sediments. On the other hand, no *existing* impoundments should be removed without a study of the probable results of such removal. The desirable effect of cooler water, for example, should be balanced against the possible undesirable result of added sediment load to the stream. An example of such a result was the great load of sand and silt carried down the Pigeon River upon failure of a dam on May 15, 1957. According to some observers, many spawning beds were smothered by the sediment, and recovery was slow, and perhaps is not yet complete. An attempt to avoid another failure of this same dam in 1984 resulted in a disastrous fish kill. The water level of the impoundment was being lowered in order to make needed repairs on the gates of the dam. The release of the water was to be controlled so that lake-bottom sediments would not be brought into the stream, but something went wrong, and huge amounts of organic sediment were washed into the Pigeon. Another possible result of dam removal that may be considered undesirable by some fishermen is the introduction of anadromous fish into waters now restricted to resident trout.

Reactivation of existing hydro dams generally is bad news for the trout fisherman. The regulation of streamflow for power production destroys the natural character of the river and may prove inconvenient or even disastrous to wading fishermen.

Saving the Bed and Banks

The character of the bed and banks of a trout stream affects its value as trout habitat and its attractiveness to the fisherman. Experiments have shown that an increase of sand sediment bed load in a trout stream can reduce the trout population to less than half its normal abundance (Alexander and Hansen 1983). Discharge of sand and silt into streams by road building, ditch digging, and other earth-moving construction is a threat to trout streams that can easily be spotted by any fisherman. This kind of activity should be reported immediately, because the damage may occur very quickly. Call first on your local town and county officials, but also notify the nearest regional office of the DNR.

Another result of man's intrusion on the land, generally unwelcome to most fishermen, is the urbanization of the stream banks. Clusters of riverside homes and cottages detract from the wilderness that many consider an essential ingredient of an attractive trout stream. Greenbelt zoning regulations now in force on the Au Sable and other Michigan streams require that a strip of natural vegetation be maintained along the river's edge. Minimum width of lots and setback restrictions for homes and waste disposal fields are also in effect. These regulations should help reduce the impact of further development on the streams. Trout fishermen, above all others, should welcome and comply with these rules.

Littering of bed and banks by users of Michigan trout streams is still a problem, although the litter has been substantially reduced by the state law eliminating "throw-away" bottles and cans. Trout fishermen can help resolve this problem not only by refraining from discarding any material along the rivers themselves, but also by picking up and disposing of litter discarded by others.

Intense use of a stream by campers, canoers, and fishermen can also cause damage to the riverbed and riverbanks. Tramping of the banks on entering or leaving the stream can shove great quantities of sand into the stream and leave the banks exposed to further erosion. Even more serious is the destruction of stream banks by off-road vehicles. The DNR has attacked these problems by moving the state forest campgrounds away from the stream banks, constructing boat ramps for launching canoes, building stairways down high sandy banks, and prohibiting motorized vehicles on streamside trails. However, none of these measures will help unless we who use the streams treat them as the valuable and fragile resource we know them to be.

Resident Trout versus Salmon and Steelhead

The introduction of salmon into classic trout waters is a controversial issue that has not been entirely resolved. Many trout fishermen contend that the competition of the salmon damages the resident trout fishery and attracts crowds of careless fishermen who destroy trout habitat, trespass on private property, and generally make life miserable for the dedicated trout angler. Others argue that the salmon fisherman should have equal rights with those who prefer trout, that the salmon fishery brings in millions of dollars of revenue to the state and local communities, and that the salmon and salmon fishers do no great damage to the trout fishery. The controversy is mainly about the Pacific salmon, as the Atlantic salmon are not yet well established in streams of the Lower Peninsula, and many dedicated trout fishermen would welcome the chance to fish for *Salmo salar*. I confess to a bias in favor of the resident trout fishery and would like to see the salmon, at least the Pacific salmon, confined to the lower reaches of the streams.

Trout fishermen generally are less critical of the steelhead competing with the resident trout, for, after all, the steelhead is a trout, and many a dry-fly enthusiast is happy to fish for steelhead in season. However, it appears that the best steelhead streams generally do not have the best resident trout fishery, and it may prove desirable to manage some streams, such as the upper Au Sable and upper Manistee, for resident trout, and others, such as the Little Manistee, for steelhead.

Get Expert Help

If you are not sure that the activity you want to protest, or the action you want to promote, is pertinent to the welfare of the trout stream, get help from the experts. The state of Michigan is fortunate in having some of the world's best fisheries biologists, and these experts can give you the information you need to keep your efforts on the target. A call to any of the field offices of the DNR will get you the name and phone number of the person best able to answer your questions.

In summary, what I am suggesting is that trout fishermen act as an advance guard to protect our trout streams. The people in state and local agencies designated to protect Michigan's water resources generally are doing the best they can, but a limited budget spreads their ranks very thin. Also, they are subject to pressure from all sides and must try to balance the legitimate needs of diverse interests. Trout fishermen can train themselves to recognize potential threats to their favorite streams and report such threats to responsible government agencies. Also, they can make sure that, when diverse arguments are heard, the needs of the trout fishery are among those considered.

Other Allies

There are three organizations that are working with you to preserve and improve the trout fishing resource. Trout Unlimited (TU) is dedicated to conservation of the trout fishery and seeks the support of all trout fishermen—bait, fly, and spin fishermen. The Federation of Fly Fishers (FFF) seeks the support of all fly-fishermen, whether they fish for trout or any other species. Michigan United Conservation Clubs (MUCC) seek, among other conservation goals, to protect the state's waters from misuse that will endanger fish and wildlife. Members of MUCC usually are also members of local conservation clubs, but individual membership is also available. Each of these organizations provides its members with magazines of outstanding quality that alone are worth the price of the annual dues.

Membership in Trout Unlimited costs $15.00 a year. Write to:

> Trout Unlimited
> P.O. Box 1944
> Washington, DC 20013

Membership in the Federation of Fly Fishers costs $20.00 a year. Write to:

> Federation of Fly Fishers
> P.O. Box 1088
> West Yellowstone, MT 59758

Membership in Michigan United Conservation Clubs costs $20.00 a year. Write to:

> Michigan United Conservation Clubs
> P.O. Box 30235
> Lansing, MI 48909

How to Use This Guide

Probably most fishermen who read this guide have fished one or more of the streams described here. Some may have yet to enjoy fishing any of these streams, and a few fortunate ones may have fished them all. In any event, I suggest that you first read the entire book to find out which of the streams are most likely to provide the kind of fishing that appeals to you. When you have chosen the stream or streams you intend to fish, you can use the same selective process to determine the sites on those streams best suited to your style of fishing.

The next thing to do, of course, is get to the stream. For each river there is a section of text that introduces the location map. Here you will find detailed directions for reaching each site, and these directions are keyed to the location map. On your first trip to these sites it is helpful to have a companion in your car—one person to drive and one to read the directions and consult the map. If you must go it alone, do not try to read directions and look at the map while driving. You are likely to end up in the ditch.

Once you have arrived at the site, look up the map and description of that site. Note the condition of the stream. Does it appear unusually high and turbid or low and clear? Remember that wading conditions vary with the stage of the river. When you are satisfied that all is as it should be, start fishing.

Michigan's Au Sable River

Michigan's Au Sable River probably is the best brown trout water in the Great Lakes region, and it may be the best east of the Rockies. The flies-only section of the river, sometimes called the "Holy Water," is ideal fly water, with good insect hatches and excellent trout populations—all stream bred. Most of it is shallow enough for easy wading, has a firm gravel bottom, and is wide enough that you can cast a fly without hanging up on streamside vegetation. The velocity of flow is only moderate, so you can wade upstream or down, depending on your energy and inclination.

The Au Sable flows through the town of Grayling on I-75, about 140 miles north of Lansing and 80 miles south of the Mackinac Bridge. It is a small south-flowing brook until it reaches Grayling, where it turns eastward and is joined by the East Branch to become a river of respectable size. The river continues eastward about 115 river miles (along the meanders of the stream) to Lake Huron.

From Grayling to Burton's Landing, about 6 river miles, much of the river bottom is sand, and some parts are too deep to wade. Trout populations are low in this part of the river, and fishing pressure is light most of the season. However, during the so-called caddis hatch (*Hexagenia limbata*), some very large trout are caught in this section.

The Holy Water section of the river begins at Burton's Landing and continues downstream about 8 river miles to Wakeley Bridge. In this section, the river gradient is steeper, the flow a little faster, and trout populations much greater than in the upstream reaches. This section is fished more than any other part of the river. No-kill regulations began on this flies-only section of the Au Sable in 1989. Fishing pressure has declined somewhat with the new regulations. The population of brown trout over 12 inches long increased slightly during the next three years but numbers of smaller fish remained about the same. The population of brook trout over 8 inches showed little change. The response of trout populations to the new regulations will be carefully monitored to determine the long-term effects. Meanwhile, the Holy Water continues to yield excellent fishing with good fly hatches throughout the season.

It may be of interest to translate the population data to fishing opportunity on the Holy Water. For example, in 1992 there were about 50 brown trout over 12 inches long per hectare in this water. With an average width of 100 feet, a fisherman could present his fly to fifty brown trout over 12 inches while wading a thousand feet up or down the river.

From Wakeley Bridge downstream to McMasters Bridge is a 9-mile stretch of extremely variable character. It begins with fast water and gravel and clay bottom, then flows slowly through the "Stillwater," where the bottom is mostly sand and banks are low.

The flies-only water on the Au Sable near Louie's Landing

The South Branch enters the Au Sable in the upper part of the Stillwater. Below the Stillwater the river picks up speed again and flows in gravel riffles to McMasters Bridge. Fishing from boats is popular in this part of the river between Wakeley and McMasters Bridge because much of it cannot be safely waded. Fishing pressure generally is relatively light.

Below McMasters Bridge, the Au Sable takes on a "big river" character, flowing alternately in deep sandy pools and shallow gravel riffles. Although some of the riffles can be waded, most of the fishing here is done by boat.

Canoe traffic on the Au Sable is heavy, especially on weekends, but the fisherman who is on the river early in the morning or late in the evening usually will see few canoes. He will also see relatively few other fishermen. Canoe traffic drops off at every take-out point below Grayling. Less than half the canoes leaving the liveries in Grayling continue beyond the take-out point at Stephan Bridge. The few who continue beyond Wakeley Bridge are mostly campers—Boy Scouts and Girl Scouts and other similar groups.

Although best known as a brown-trout stream, the Au Sable also supports a substantial population of brook trout. They are especially eager to take a fly but are mostly small fish. An occasional rainbow is caught, and recent surveys show these are on the increase, particularly in the Stephan Bridge area.

The Au Sable was not always a trout stream. Before about 1890 grayling were the sport fish of the Au Sable system. Early lumbermen called the grayling "white trout" or "Crawford County trout," but in 1874 the fish were identified as grayling. Local residents then changed the name of their town from Crawford to Grayling. The first brook trout to enter the Au Sable system reportedly were taken from the Jordan River and planted in the East Branch of the Au Sable by Rube Babbit in the 1880s. Rainbow trout had been planted somewhat earlier and browns came shortly after. Grayling became scarce soon after the trout appeared, but few of the old-time residents blame the trout for this. Apparently the grayling was less tolerant of changing conditions than the trout, and it is doubtful if the grayling could have survived even if trout had not entered the river. The last grayling reported caught in the Au Sable mainstream was taken by Dan Stephan in 1908 about 3 miles above McMasters Bridge.

The Au Sable is excellent trout habitat because it is relatively steady in flow, has generally cool summer water temperatures, and, in most of the upper river, ample clean gravel spawning beds. About 85 percent of the flow of the upper Au Sable is from groundwater discharge, so the stream is not subject to large changes in stage or velocity. In an average year it is only about 1 foot higher at high water than at normal low flow. Unusually great snowmelt or heavy rains can bring this up a bit, but the Au Sable is generally a remarkably steady stream. As pointed out earlier, however, a rise of even 6 inches can make wading much more difficult.

The groundwater inflow also helps to keep the Au Sable cool in summer. Water temperatures sometimes go higher than 75 degrees F in the sandy area below Grayling, but the water rarely gets that warm in the flies-only section. Brook trout, the least tolerant of warm water, seem to thrive in this section of the river.

There are excellent hatches of almost all Michigan flies on the Au Sable. Hatches are especially good on the flies-only section, except for the drake and *Hexagenia* hatches. These hatches are better in the sand and silt sections of the river, both above and below the flies-only water.

Accommodations

The fisherman who comes to the Au Sable will have no trouble finding a place to stay, provided that reservations are made far enough in advance. Many excellent motels are in Grayling, and there are plenty of restaurants also. Streamside accommodations are available at Gate's Au Sable Lodge just downstream from Stephan Bridge.

For the campers there are five state forest campgrounds on the river between Grayling and McMasters Bridge. Two of these are on the flies-only section of the river.

Many stores and some canoe liveries in Grayling stock fishing tackle of all kinds. Some of the lodges and resorts on the river and rural general stores also stock fishing tackle, especially trout flies. Some of the best flytiers in the country live in Grayling, and excellent flies are always available. The storekeepers and other local residents in Grayling are friendly and will gladly furnish you helpful information on the current hatches and fishing conditions.

For the fisherman who wants to fish the lower unwadable waters, there are expert guides with Au Sable riverboats at your

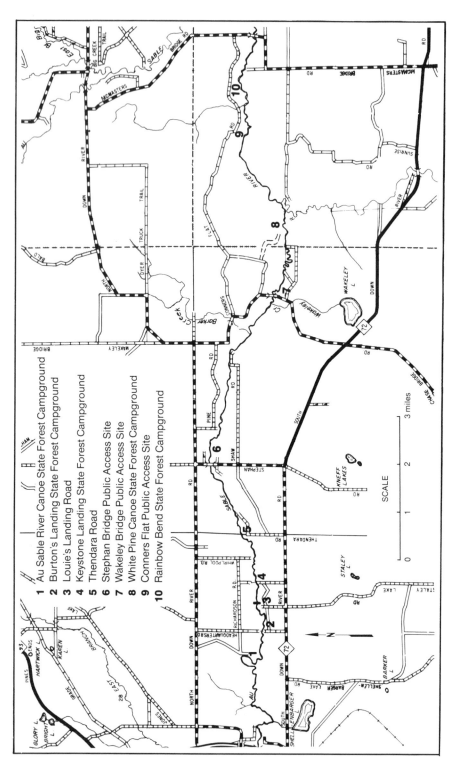

1   Au Sable River Canoe State Forest Campground
2   Burton's Landing State Forest Campground
3   Louie's Landing Road
4   Keystone Landing State Forest Campground
5   Thendara Road
6   Stephan Bridge Public Access Site
7   Wakeley Bridge Public Access Site
8   White Pine Canoe State Forest Campground
9   Conners Flat Public Access Site
10 Rainbow Bend State Forest Campground

SCALE

0   1   2   3 miles

Fig. 1.   Location map of the Upper Au Sable River

service. The Au Sable riverboat was designed expressly for trout fishermen on the Au Sable, but it is now used on many Michigan streams. You can cover a lot of water in a day's fishing in one of these. Float fishing is especially helpful to those fishermen whose physical condition no longer permits them to wade the stream.

Maps of the Au Sable

The location map (fig. 1) shows the stream channel and public roads leading to the river. Ten numbered fishing sites also are shown on this map. For each of these ten sites there is a larger-scale map showing the river channel in greater detail. Use the location map to find your way to the fishing site and the larger-scale map to show you the fishing conditions you will find at each site.

To get to these sites you can drive east from Grayling on either the North Down River Road (County 608) or the South Down River Road (M-72). Site 1 can be reached only from the North Down River Road. Sites 2, 3, 4, and 5 can be reached only from the South Down River Road. Sites 6 through 10 can be reached from either road. Most of the roads leading north from the South Down River Road and south from the North Down River Road end at the river. Outside the town of Grayling, only Stephan Bridge Road, Wakeley Bridge Road, and McMasters Bridge Road cross the river in the area covered in figure 1.

Directions for reaching each of the sites follow. Starting point for each is the town of Grayling.

To get to the Au Sable River Canoe Campground (site 1), take the business route of I-75 (McClellen Street) in Grayling north to the north city limits just south of the Elmwood Cemetery. Turn right (east) on the county road here and continue east across the bridge over the East Branch of the Au Sable. At this bridge you will see the old fish hatchery on your right (south) side of the road. Continue on this blacktop county road past the overpass on I-75. About one-half mile beyond the overpass the blacktop swings to the left (north) for a mile and then turns right (east) again. Continue east on this road, known as the North Down River Road, 2 more miles to the intersection with Headquarters Road (fig. 2), a graded road that leads off to the right (south). Go south on Headquarters Road about 1.2 miles to a dirt road leading off to the right (west). There is a sign marking the road to the campground at this turnoff. Follow this road about three-fourths of a mile to the campground.

To get to Burton's Landing Campground (site 2), take the business route of I-75 south from downtown Grayling past the bridge over the Au Sable River to the intersection with the South Down River Road. The South Down River Road is the eastern section of M-72. Turn left at the stoplight onto the South Down River Road and go east on this road exactly 3 miles to Burton's Landing Road (fig. 3). Turn left (north) on Burton's Landing Road and go about 0.4 mile to the dirt road leading off to the right (east) to the campground.

Louie's Landing (site 3) is the next public access site downstream from Burton's. Continue east on the South Down River Road (M-72) exactly one-half mile past Burton's Landing Road to Louie's Landing Road (fig. 4). Turn left (north) on this graded road and go about one-half mile to the river.

Next downstream is Keystone Landing Campground (site 4). Continue east on the South Down River Road one-half mile beyond Louie's Landing Road to Keystone Landing Road (fig. 5). Turn left (north) on this road and go about one-half mile to the camp road leading off to the right (east) to the campground.

Thendara Road (site 5) is 1 mile east of Keystone Landing Road. Turn left (north) off the South Down River Road onto Thendara Road (fig. 6) and go about 0.8 mile to the river.

To get to Stephan Bridge Public Access Site (site 6), continue east on the South Down River Road about 1.4 miles past Thendara Road to Stephan Bridge Road (fig. 7). A general store selling groceries and fishing tackle is at this intersection. Turn left (north) on Stephan Bridge Road and go about 1.5 miles to a dirt road leading off to the right (east). Follow this road east to the access site on the south bank of the river.

Wakeley Bridge Road intersects the South Down River Road about 2.8 miles east of Stephan Bridge Road. A general store is at this intersection also. Turn left (north) on Wakeley Bridge Road (fig. 8) and go about 2 miles to a dirt road leading off to the right (east). There is a sign at the turnoff indicating the road to the public access site (site 7). Follow this road about 0.2 mile to the river.

The White Pine Canoe Campground is about 1.6 miles east of Wakeley Bridge (straight-line distance). Drive north from Wakeley

Bridge on Wakeley Bridge Road about 0.3 mile to a dirt road leading off to the right (east). Turn right on this road and follow the main-traveled track as it winds generally eastward (fig. 9). Ignore the private roads turning off to riverside cabins. At about 0.8 mile from the turnoff the road turns sharply north and just beyond this turn there is another dirt road leading off to the right (east). Turn right on this road and follow it as it leads generally east, south, and east, again ignoring the side roads and sticking to the main-traveled track. About 1.3 miles from this last turnoff you will come to the campground parking lot on the right (south) side of the road. A car compass is a big help in following the roads in this kind of backcountry. There are no signs whatever to guide you to the campground (site 8).

The public access site at Conners Flat (site 9) is about 1.8 miles west of McMasters Bridge (fig. 10). McMasters Bridge Road (County F-97) intersects the South Down River Road (M-72) about 6.2 miles east of Wakeley Bridge Road. Turn left (north) on McMasters Bridge Road (County F-97) and go 4.1 miles to the bridge, then continue north of the bridge 0.4 mile to Conners Flat Road, a dirt road leading off to the left (west). Follow this winding road generally westward about 2.2 miles to the intersection with another dirt road leading off to the left (south). There is a sign marked "Conners Flat" at this intersection. Turn left (south) and go about 0.2 mile to the public access site on the river.

Rainbow Bend Campground (site 10) is about 0.7 mile downstream (east of) Conners Flat (fig. 11). Starting again at McMasters Bridge, go north 0.4 mile to Conners Flat Road leading off to the left (west). Turn left (west) on this dirt road and go about 1.5 miles to a road turning off to the left (south). There is no sign at this turnoff, but the tree trunks on both sides are sprayed with a band of yellow paint. Turn left on this road and follow it generally southeast about 0.35 mile to the parking area near the campground.

There is a public access site just south of McMasters Bridge on the downstream (east) side. This is not a numbered site but it is a good spot to take out your boat after float fishing the Stillwater.

Other access sites on the Au Sable, accessible from the North Down River Road, include the south end of Whirlpool Road and two sites managed by Trout Unlimited—one upstream from Stephan Bridge Road and one upstream from Wakeley Bridge Road.

Site No. 1. Au Sable River Canoe State Forest Campground

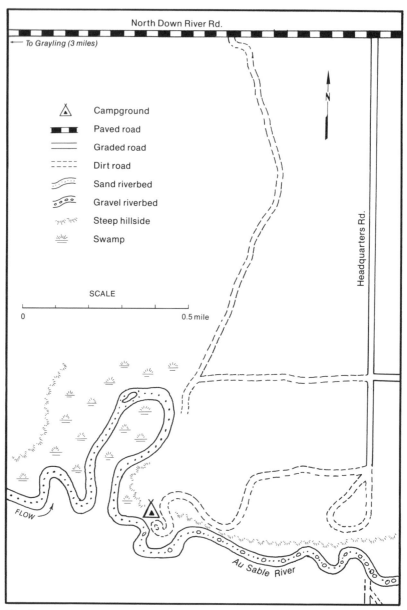

North Down River Rd.

← To Grayling (3 miles)

Campground
Paved road
Graded road
Dirt road
Sand riverbed
Gravel riverbed
Steep hillside
Swamp

SCALE

0   0.5 mile

Headquarters Rd.

N

FLOW

Au Sable River

Fig. 2

This campground usually is more popular with canoeists than with trout fishermen. However, when the caddis hatch is on in late June this part of the river yields some very large fish. The so-called caddis is, of course, the large mayfly, *Hexagenia limbata.*

Fishing the caddis hatch is a chancey thing, and I have spent many a night on this part of the river waiting in vain for a hatch or spinner fall. But when it is good it is very, very good. To hear the splash of a taking trout, feel the tug as you set the hook, and the throb of a heavy fish as you play him to net, often in pitch blackness, is an experience worth all the fruitless nights.

The Au Sable is about 100 feet wide here and 3 to 6 feet deep. The bottom is mostly sand, with scattered patches of gravel. Silt and muck deposits, sometimes called "loonsilt," are common along the banks. The riverbanks are alternately low and swampy and high and sandy. The low banks are lined with brush and swamp conifers, the high banks with upland pine and aspen. The river can be waded with caution at normal stages, but you can overtop your waders at mid-channel in many places. The river flow is slow to moderate, so you can wade upstream without too much trouble, as long as you keep in the shallower parts. There is plenty of room to cast a fly without hanging up on streamside vegetation.

The usual strategy in fishing the caddis hatch is to choose your spot well before dark. Find a place where there is good cover along the bank. Drowned logs, snags, tree stumps, and roots usually shelter some good fish. Make sure you can wade out to fish this cover without disturbing the feeding trout. Now wade back to the bank and pick out a comfortable spot to sit and wait for the hatch. If other fishermen come along they will usually respect your prior claim and move upstream or down a respectable distance from you. It is considered very bad form to crowd a fisherman who has taken up his place before you.

Site No. 2. Burton's Landing State Forest Campground

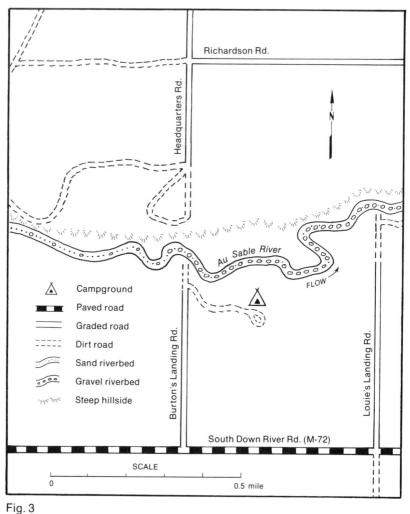

Richardson Rd.

Headquarters Rd.

N

Au Sable River

FLOW

△ Campground
Paved road
Graded road
Dirt road
Sand riverbed
Gravel riverbed
Steep hillside

Burton's Landing Rd.

Louie's Landing Rd.

South Down River Rd. (M-72)

SCALE

0   0.5 mile

Fig. 3

The upper flies-only, no-kill water begins at Burton's Landing. Just before you get to the river there is a road leading off to the right (east) that takes you first to a parking area and then on to the campground. There is space for twelve camping parties here, and spaces usually are available except on some of the busiest weekends. Trout fishermen find easy access to the river from this campground, and the river here holds some fine brown trout. Nevertheless, this campground is generally not so popular with trout fishermen as the Keystone Landing Campground, next downstream.

The river is 80 to 90 feet wide here and 2 to 4 feet deep, with some deeper holes. Bottom is mostly gravel going downstream from the landing. Going upstream, you run into more sandy bottom. Velocity is moderate. Wading is fairly easy at normal flows and there is plenty of room for fly casting. Trout cover is chiefly drowned logs along the banks. The riverbank on the south side is generally less than 5 feet high. On the north side the bank is generally higher and sandier. Coniferous trees, brush, and some hardwoods line the banks.

The north bank upstream from the landing all the way to the canoe camp is state land, and the south bank is state land from the landing downstream about one-fourth mile. The rest of the river frontage is all private land.

Bait and spin fishermen can fish upstream from the landing under standard regulations. Downstream from the landing, the fishing is restricted to flies only and all trout must be returned to the water.

Site No. 3. Louie's Landing Road

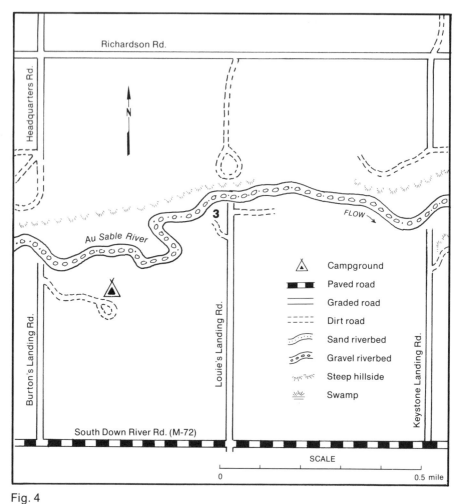

Fig. 4

This is not a designated public access site, but there is room to turn around and park your car on the upstream (west) side of the road. This is all private property, both sides of the river, upstream and down. To fish this part of the river without trespassing on private property you will have to wade upstream, either at the start or the finish of your fishing. Upstream wading is not too difficult, as the velocity of flow is moderate, and the river is less than 4 feet deep, except for a few deeper holes. Some of the holes will overtop your waders, but these can easily be avoided. Bottom is mostly gravel, with some sand. Trout cover, mostly drowned logs and fallen trees, is abundant. The chief obstacles to wading fishermen, especially at night, are the drowned logs and underwater stumps, some at mid-channel. These can trip you up or puncture your waders.

The river channel is 90 to 100 feet wide here and 2 to 3 feet deep, except for the deeper holes. The riverbank on the south side is mostly 5 to 10 feet high. On the north side it is more than 20 feet high in places, low and swampy in others. Pine, spruce, and cedar trees line the lower banks, upland pine and aspen top the higher banks.

Site No. 4. Keystone Landing State Forest Campground

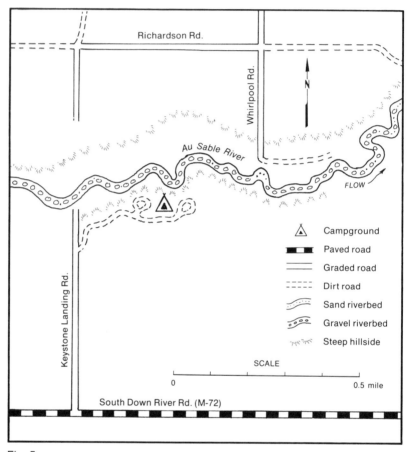

Fig. 5

Prior to 1975, this was a public access site called Highbanks, where camping was permitted. Strong friendships were forged among the campers in those early years, but most of the old Highbanks comrades are no longer known to me. Some, perhaps, have already gone to those far-off celestial streams where I, too, may someday cast a fly. The campground now has eighteen spaces set well back from the river. There is also ample parking space for fishermen who are not campers.

This is superb water, with good fly hatches and excellent trout population—all stream-bred trout. Brook trout are more abundant in this part of the stream.

The river is about 100 feet wide and 2 to 4 feet deep, with some deeper holes. One of these deeper holes is called the "Whirlpool," located, appropriately enough, at the south end of Whirlpool Road, one-half mile downstream from Keystone Landing. If you approach too close to this hole from the upstream side the shifting sands will undermine your footing and you will get a dunking. Many a fisherman has had to swim for it in the Whirlpool.

The river bottom is mostly gravel with some sand. Stream velocity is moderate, and wading is fairly easy if you keep out of the deeper holes. However, the night fisherman should watch out for an occasional boulder and some log rafts anchored in the stream to serve as trout cover. Other cover is provided by drowned logs and snags along both banks.

Highbanks got its name from the predominantly high south bank. The north bank is generally low, and, in places, swampy. Except for the grassy areas fronting some of the streamside cabins, the banks are lined with cedar, pine, aspen, oak, and some brush. Two stairways at the campground allow easy access to the river. Fishermen should use these to avoid damage to the vulnerable sandy banks.

This is one of the heavily fished areas of the river, yet it continues to yield good fishing, year after year. Again, if you fish early or late you may sometimes have the river to yourself. Fishing early and late also avoids most of the canoe traffic, which is especially heavy on weekends. However, in the early season, when most of the good hatches are in the afternoon, you will have to take your chances on the canoes.

The south bank from Keystone Landing downstream to the Whirlpool is all state land. The north bank is all private.

Site No. 5. Thendara Road

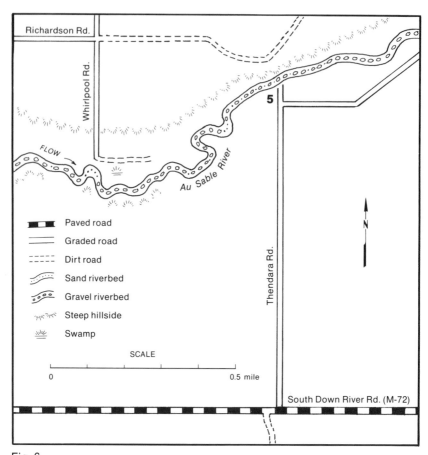

Richardson Rd.

Whirlpool Rd.

FLOW

Au Sable River

5

Thendara Rd.

N

Paved road	
Graded road	
Dirt road	
Sand riverbed	
Gravel riverbed	
Steep hillside	
Swamp	

SCALE

0   0.5 mile

South Down River Rd. (M-72)

Fig. 6

Although no public land is at this site other than the roadway, you can enter the river without trespassing at the road's end. You will find plenty of room to park your car and room to turn around when you are ready to go home.

Going upstream, the river is 90 to 100 feet wide and 2 to 4 feet deep, with some holes 6 feet deep. Bottom is gravel and sand. You can wade upstream against the current, avoiding the deeper holes, and fish the most productive water. Good trout cover is provided by logjams, snags, and stumps, and by the depth of water itself. Once you get above Camp Wa Wa Sum, you will see few cabins or homes on the river. Some good brown trout feed in this part of the river, and fishing pressure usually is moderate.

Going downstream, the river is 100 to 120 feet wide and 1 to 3 feet deep, with a few holes that will overtop your waders. With the shallower depth, wading is easier downstream than up, but more cabins and homes line the river here, and trout cover is not so plentiful. Bottom is sand and gravel. A little more than one-half mile downstream from the road is a deep hole on the outside of a sharp bend that usually holds some large trout.

There is a high sandy bank on the north side of the river opposite the end of the road and some high banks on both sides of the river upstream. Downstream, the banks are generally low and swampy.

Site No. 6. Stephan Bridge Public Access Site

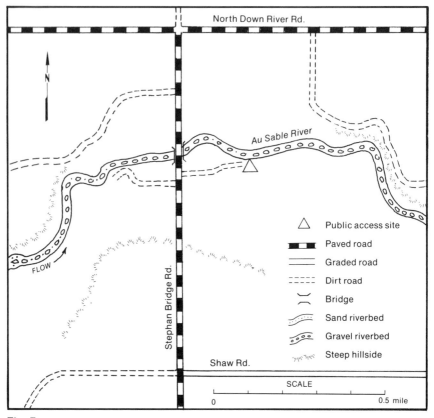

Fig. 7

This public access site is much used as a take-out landing for rented canoes, but it is also quite popular with fishermen. Camping is not permitted at this site. It is located on the south bank of the river a few hundred feet downstream (east) of the bridge. Gate's Au Sable Lodge, on the south bank just downstream from the bridge, is popular with trout fishermen.

The river is 100 to 120 feet wide here and 2 to 3 feet deep, with some deeper holes both upstream and down. Bottom is mostly gravel with some sand. Velocity is moderate. Wading is generally easy, and there is plenty of room to cast a fly. Banks are mostly low on both sides of the river and are wooded with cedar, spruce, and pine. Drowned logs and snags give trout cover, generally better along the north bank than the south.

The excellent fly hatches, good trout populations, and easy wading make this reach a favorite of the fly fishermen, and it is usually heavily fished. The intense canoe activity in this take-out place is something of a handicap to fishermen, but much of this can be avoided by wading a few hundred feet upstream or down from the landing.

It is a good idea to park your car well back from the river so you do not get in the way of cars and trailers that haul the canoes back to the liveries. The site is equipped with outdoor toilets. Except for the public access site, the river banks on both sides are all private land.

A 1982 survey by the DNR showed about 50 percent brown trout, 35 percent rainbows, and 15 percent brookies here. The percentage of rainbows has increased substantially in recent years, and is greater than in any other part of the upper Au Sable.

Site No. 7. Wakeley Bridge Public Access Site

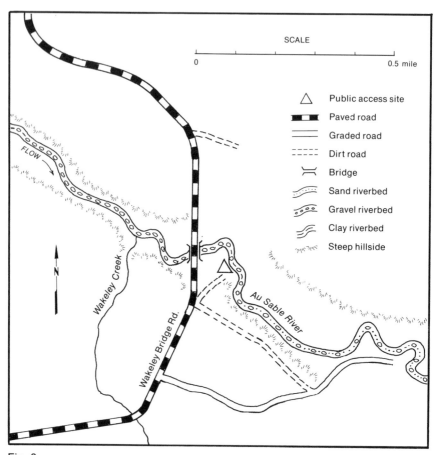

Fig. 8

This public access site just downstream from Wakeley Bridge is not much used by fishermen. The fast current and slippery clay bottom in places make wading extremely difficult. Cleated soles and a wading staff probably would help. There are some large trout in this water to tempt those with the strength and courage to fish here.

There is a fork in the access road, with signs showing the left fork leading to the canoe landing and the right fork to the parking area. Take the right fork, park your car in the designated area, and walk down the path to the river.

The river is relatively narrow here—60 to 90 feet wide—and 2 to 4 feet deep, with some holes that may overtop your waders. Bottom is mostly gravel and hard, slippery clay. As you go downstream the bottom gets sandier as you approach the Stillwater. The banks are low, forested with hardwood, conifer, and some brush. Trout cover is sparse. Except for the public access site, this is all private property.

You can fish with bait, spinning lure, or fly here, under standard regulations, as long as you stay below the bridge. Upstream from the bridge, the water is restricted to the special regulations flies-only, no-kill rules.

Site No. 8. White Pine Canoe State Forest Campground

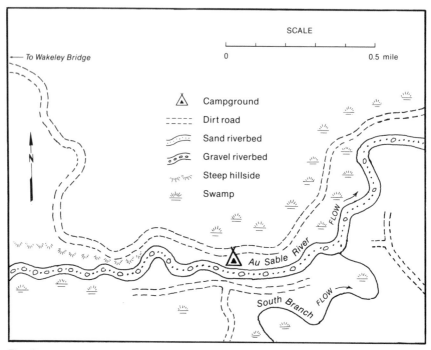

SCALE

To Wakeley Bridge

0   0.5 mile

▲ Campground
- - - - Dirt road
～～ Sand riverbed
○ ○ ○ Gravel riverbed
Steep hillside
Swamp

N

▲ Au Sable River

FLOW

South Branch   FLOW

Fig. 9

This campground is designed primarily for canoe campers and is not much used by fishermen. You cannot drive into the campground, but you can park your car in the designated parking area and walk about 60 yards to the river.

This is the start of that part of the river called the Stillwater. The flow is slow to moderate. The bottom is sand, soft mud, and some gravel and boulders. The river is about 150 feet wide here. It is too deep for easy wading, overtopping your waders in many places. The left bank (north) is 5 to 8 feet high at the campground, forested with pine and oak and some brush. The south bank is generally lower. Cover is sparse in this part of the river.

Like all the Stillwater, this reach of the river has excellent hatches of Michigan caddis (*Hexagenia*) in late June or early July. It can be fished in places by wading, but it is easier fished by boat. Standard regulations are in effect here, allowing you to fish with bait, spinning lure, or fly. Fishing bait in this water will result in the occasional catch of a round whitefish, *Prosopium cylindracum.* Like trout, these fish belong to the family Salmonidae.

Site No. 9. Conners Flat Public Access Site

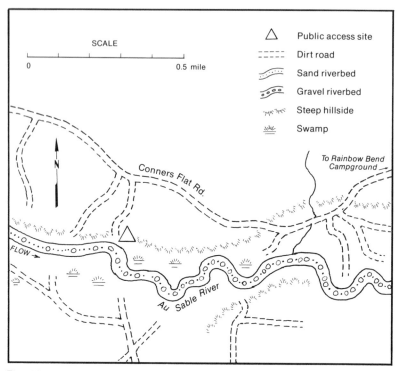

SCALE

0   0.5 mile

△   Public access site
- - - - -   Dirt road
～～⋯⋯   Sand riverbed
～∘∘∘∘   Gravel riverbed
ᵧₙᵥ ᵧₙᵥ   Steep hillside
⸲ᴸᵉ   Swamp

N

Conners Flat Rd.

To Rainbow Bend
Campground →

FLOW →

Au Sable River

Fig. 10

This public access site is on the Stillwater. There is a parking area, and toilets and a trash barrel are provided, but no drinking-water supply. The river is about 150 feet wide. You can wade with caution along the banks in places, but the river at mid-channel will overtop your waders. Like most of the Stillwater the river is easier fished by boat.

The bottom is sand and gravel and mud, with a few boulders. The gravel may be a thin veneer over sand, as it feels quite soft underfoot in places. The flow is slow to moderate. The north bank at the access site is 3 to 4 feet high, sparsely forested with oak, maple, and popple. The south bank is low and swampy, with a dense cover of cedar, spruce, and popple. Trout cover is somewhat sparse. However, some whopper trout are in this part of the river.

Site No. 10. Rainbow Bend State Forest Campground

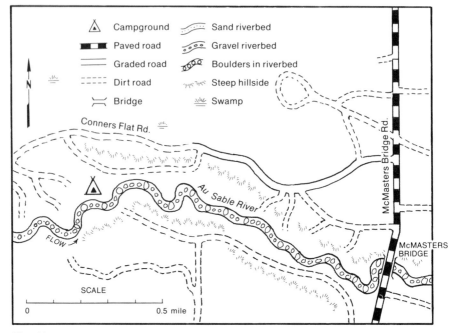

Fig. 11

This campground is located just downstream from the Stillwater. Cars are not allowed in the camping area, but a parking area is provided, with a path leading about 150 yards to the river. The campground has spaces for five camping parties, with additional spaces for group camping. Like all state forest campgrounds in Michigan, the camp is equipped with a water supply, picnic tables, and toilets.

The river is about 100 feet wide and over your wader tops in places at mid-channel. You can wade with caution at normal low flows in places near the banks. At mid-channel the river is generally too fast and too deep for safe wading. The bottom is gravel, sand, and boulders, and the footing is not too secure.

The north bank at the campground is 5 to 10 feet high, with an open forest of oak and maple. The south bank is low and swampy, covered with cedar and popple. Trout cover is sparse.

This is not easy water to fish, but there are some good trout to be caught here.

South Branch of the Au Sable

The South Branch of the Au Sable is the favorite of many anglers who are especially interested in catching big browns. It is not always an easy river to fish, however. In the early season, and after heavy rains at any season, the river flows fast, high, and murky, and the rounded cobbles and boulders are slippery. I can recall only three times that I have slipped and fallen while wading a trout stream, and two of these were on the South Branch.

The flow of the South Branch is much more variable than that of either the mainstream or the North Branch. Consequently, wading and fishing conditions change greatly from day to day. The reach you waded with ease one day may be totally unwadable another, and the cover that harbored some huge trout on one day may be left high and dry after a long drought. The water is clear at normal low flows but becomes so cloudy after heavy rains that you may not be able to see the deep holes that will overtop your waders.

Trout populations generally are lower on the South Branch than on the mainstream or North Branch (Gowing and Alexander 1980), but fishermen who know the river do well on the South Branch. Fishing pressure is heavy on the South Branch during the drake hatch and even heavier during the *Hexagenia* hatch. A survey by Gaylord Alexander (1974) showed that evening fishing in the Mason Tract of the South Branch increased from about 75 angler hours per day in the first week of June to about 375 angler hours per day in the fourth week of that month. In the first week in July fishing had dropped off to about 270 angler hours per day. Before and after these hatches of the large mayflies, fishing pressure is light to moderate. In general, the farther you walk from the access roads, the better your chances of fishing alone on the river. But you also run a better chance of getting lost going to and from these remote spots.

From its source in Lake St. Helen to Roscommon, the South Branch is too warm to support a good trout fishery, and it does not become a really first-class trout water until it reaches Chase Bridge, about 6 river miles below this city. From Chase Bridge all the way down to Smith Bridge, about 12 river miles, the South Branch is classic fly water.

This stretch of river, called the Mason Tract after the donor, George Mason, has an interesting history. According to Mrs. Margaret Jenson (1982), most of the Mason Tract was formerly a club property owned by a Mr. Downey and several others. When the club broke up Mr. Downey purchased all the forties fronting the river. Mr. Downey died in 1921, and several years later his widow sold the property to her nephew, Mr. Durant, who built the ill-fated "Castle" on the South Branch below Chase Bridge. Mr. Durant's widow, in turn, sold the land to George Mason and D. B. Lee, and D. B. Lee's widow sold Lee's share to Mr. Mason.

The South Branch of the Au Sable at Dogtown

In accordance with Mr. Mason's wishes, this tract, now state property, remains free of all development except for a simple log chapel and one campground. The river is 50 to 100 feet wide here and mostly 2 to 4 feet deep at mid-channel, with many holes over your wader tops and a few over your head, even at low water. The streambed is mostly gravel, with sand and muck along the banks and in some of the deeper holes. There are large boulders in places and some patches of hard, slippery clay.

Until recent years the South Branch from Smith Bridge to the mouth, about 5 river miles, flowed through private property, and there was no public access to this part of the river except by boat. However, the state of Michigan has now acquired part of this frontage, and public access may be provided at some future date. Until that time, you can launch your boat at Smith Bridge, float down to the mouth, and then continue on down the mainstream to Conners Flat Public Access Site or Rainbow Bend Campground. Much of this lower river is too deep to wade, and some of the holes are over your head. As you approach the Stillwater section of the mainstream, the South Branch flows more slowly and the bottom is more sandy.

Bait and spin fishing is permitted above Chase Bridge, but from Chase Bridge all the way to the mouth, about 17 river miles, the South Branch is designated quality fishing water limited to fly-fishing. In addition, the 4 river miles from Chase Bridge downstream to the Lower Highbanks are designated no-kill water. All fish caught here must be returned to the river. No-kill regulations began on this part of the South Branch in 1983, six years earlier than on the Holy Water of the mainstream. In the next nine years the number of brown trout 12 inches and longer increased somewhat, but the numbers of smaller trout did not change substantially. Populations of brook trout over 8 inches varied widely but showed no definite long-term trend.

As a canoe trail, the South Branch is almost as popular as the mainstream. Liveries at Roscommon supply rental canoes and put-in and take-out service. The fisherman may find the canoes interrupt his fishing at midday, but there will be few canoes on the river in the very early morning or late evening. Not much fishing is done from boats on the South Branch, but this is one way you can fish the more remote spots without fear of getting lost. Unless you are fortunate enough to own a cabin on the South Branch below Smith

Bridge, float fishing is the only possible access to this part of the river.

From Roscommon downstream to the mouth the South Branch has enough groundwater inflow to keep the summer temperatures cool enough for trout. Like all the streams in this part of Michigan the water is hard and high in calcium and magnesium, and slightly alkaline. The supply of nutrients is adequate to support the species on which the trout feed.

The gravel bottom that predominates at mid-channel provides ample spawning beds, and the sand and muck along the banks and in the deeper holes give rise to excellent drake and *Hexagenia* hatches.

Accommodations

The city of Roscommon is a few miles southwest of the best trout water on the South Branch. Good motels and restaurants are available to fishermen here, and fishing tackle of all kinds can be bought at sporting goods and hardware stores in Roscommon.

For the campers there is one good campground in the lower end of the Mason Tract. This campground, called the Canoe Harbor Campground, has space for forty-five camping parties and additional space for group camping for canoeists.

Maps of the South Branch

The channel of the South Branch and public roads leading to the streams are shown on the location map (fig. 12).

Some of the access sites on the South Branch in the Mason Tract are hard to find, and you can spend hours of fruitless wandering on single-track roads that appear to lead off in all directions. For this reason I have included another map showing the upper (or southwestern) end of the Mason Tract in greater detail (fig. 13). This map is reproduced from topographic quadrangles and shows most of the roads and tracks along the river. This is in addition to the site maps at still larger scale.

A car compass mounted on your dash or windshield and properly compensated is a big help in driving these roads. At least you will know if you are going in the right general direction. Slow down

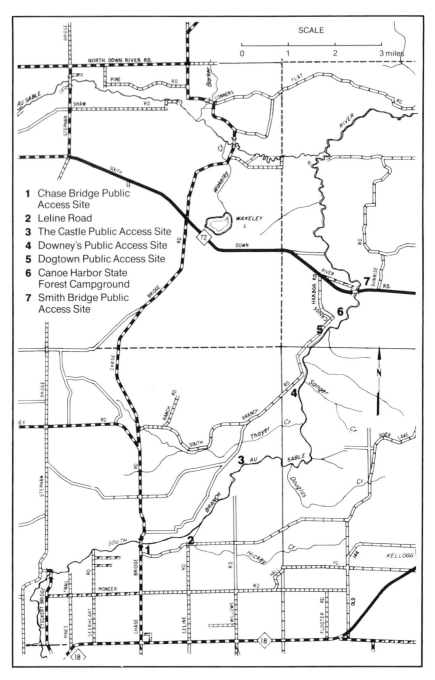

SCALE

0   1   2   3 miles

1 Chase Bridge Public
   Access Site
2 Leline Road
3 The Castle Public Access Site
4 Downey's Public Access Site
5 Dogtown Public Access Site
6 Canoe Harbor State
   Forest Campground
7 Smith Bridge Public
   Access Site

Fig. 12.   Location map of the South Branch Au Sable

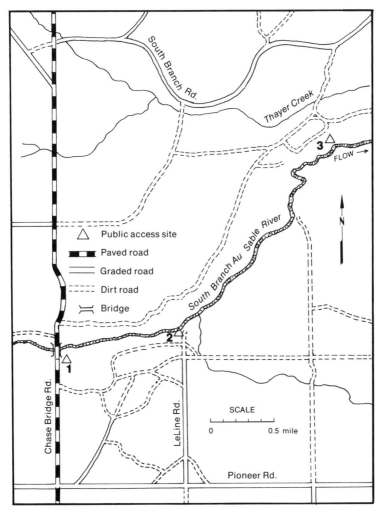

Fig. 13. Road access to sites in the Mason Tract

and give your compass time to settle after a turn. A bouncing car will have the compass pointing in all directions. Many of the roads in the Mason Tract have soft spots where you can get stuck at times, especially in dry weather.

Seven numbered access sites are shown on figure 12. Chase Bridge is a good starting point for the first three of these sites. To get to Chase Bridge, take M-18 northeast out of Roscommon and go 2.5 miles to the intersection with Chase Bridge Road. Turn left (north) on the blacktop Chase Bridge Road and go 2 miles to the bridge. Chase Bridge is site 1.

Leline Road (site 2, fig. 15) is a mile downstream (east) from Chase Bridge. Go back (south) from Chase Bridge (toward Roscommon) on Chase Bridge Road 1 mile to the intersection with Pioneer Road. Turn left (east) on this road and go 1 mile to the intersection with Leline Road. Turn left again (north) on Leline Road and go 1 mile to an intersection with an east-west dirt road. Continue straight north from this intersection and go about 0.1 mile to where the road drops sharply down a steep hill. Do not try to drive down this hill unless you have a four-wheel drive and a lot of confidence. Instead, park on the left (west) side of the road and walk down to the river. The land to the west of the road belongs to the state. East of the road the land is private, and there is a riverside lodge there.

The next site (site 3, fig. 16) is "The Castle" on the left (northwest) bank of the river in the Mason Tract. To get to the Castle go north from Chase Bridge on the blacktop Chase Bridge Road about 0.25 mile to a dirt road leading off to the right (east). Turn right on this road and you will see a large sign that says "The Mason Tract . . . Sportsman, slow your pace. . . ." This is good advice in any event, because the road is rough and narrow, and there is grass growing between the tracks. If you meet another car, one of you must find a place to pull off the road to let the other go by. When you have gone (mostly east) 0.7 mile you will come to a fork in the road not shown on the maps. Actually, it is a three-way fork. You take the middle fork going northeast, the one most traveled. Go another 0.2 mile on this middle fork and a road comes in from the right. Continue on the main-traveled road. Another 0.7 mile (1.6 miles from the turnoff from Chase Bridge Road) and you come to another fork. Take the left fork. Another 0.6 mile (2.2

miles from the turnoff) and another fork. Again, take the left fork going northeast. The right fork goes almost straight east. This is the first fork you come to that shows on the topographic map (fig. 13). Another 0.2 mile and a road comes in from the left. Continue ahead (northeast). Another 0.2 mile and a road turns off to the right (southeast). You continue on northeast another 0.3 mile to a T intersection. This is 2.9 miles from the turnoff from Chase Bridge Road.

Turn right (southeast) at this T intersection and go 0.1 mile. Here the road turns right again (southwest) and there is a parking area on the left (southeast) side of the road. Park your car here and walk down the path about 250 yards to the river at the Castle. There is an old rusty gate just to the right of the path.

If you find these detailed directions too tedious, you probably can arrive at the right spot by taking the turnoff from Chase Bridge Road and driving east and northeast on the main-traveled road 2.9 miles to the T intersection. Then turn right and go 0.1 mile to the parking area. Remember that no two odometers will read exactly alike, so you may need to make some adjustments in the mileage figures.

You can go back to the T intersection, take the north fork, and continue north and northeast to Downey's and Dogtown access sites and on to the Canoe Harbor Campground, but this is a long, rough road, and the chances of getting lost are many. For your first visits to these sites you will find it easier to start from the lower end and work south (upstream).

Use the intersection of Chase Bridge Road and M-72 (South Down River Road) as your starting point. This intersection is about 7.5 miles north (by road) from Chase Bridge and about 9.2 miles east of Grayling. To get to Canoe Harbor (site 6, fig. 19) go southeast on M-72 from Chase Bridge Road about 3.4 miles to Canoe Harbor Road. Turn right (south) on this gravel road and go 0.8 mile to the campground entrance on the left (east).

Dogtown (site 5, fig. 18) is the next access upstream from the campground. Continue south on Canoe Harbor Road. About 0.1 mile south of the campground it makes a long turn to the left (east) and continues east about 0.2 mile. The road formerly continued on east to the old campground on the river, but there is a road block here now, and you turn to the right on South Branch Road and follow this rough, rocky road south and southwest about 0.5 mile to the Dogtown parking area. Just before you get to the parking area the road goes down a steep hill, and at the bottom of the hill the road turns sharply right. The parking area is on the left (east) side of the road at the bend. Park your car here and follow the path about 80 yards down to the river.

Next upstream from Dogtown is Downey's (site 4, fig. 17). Continue southwest from Dogtown on the same road (South Branch Road) 1 mile to an intersection with a dirt road coming in from the northwest (right). The parking area for Downey's is just opposite (southeast of) this intersection. South Branch Road goes straight southwest for more than a mile from Downey's. This is the only long straight stretch on this road. Park your car in the off-road parking area and walk down the path southeast about 300 yards to the river. You will see a rock stairway and a rock wall along the riverbank.

The South Branch of the Au Sable at Smith Bridge

There are many other places in the Mason Tract where you can park your car and walk to the river. If you want to explore these be sure to carry a map and compass. Another way to explore the more remote spots is to float down from Chase Bridge. You can fish from the boat or anchor and wade the shallower reaches.

Smith Bridge Public Access Site (site 7, fig. 20) is about 0.85 mile southeast of the intersection of Canoe Harbor Road and M-72. Go southeast from this intersection on M-72 0.1 mile to a gravel road turning off to the left (northeast). Follow this road northeast and then southeast as it roughly parallels M-72 about 0.75 mile to the public access site that lies between Smith Bridge on the south and the old bridge on the north.

Site No. 1. Chase Bridge Public Access Site

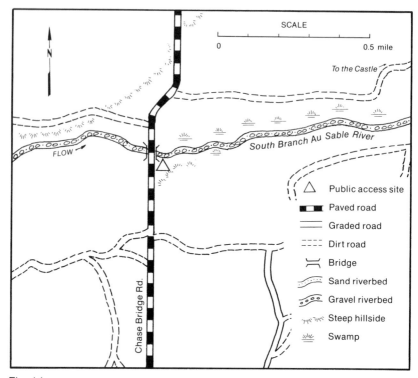

Fig. 14

Chase Bridge is the upper limit of the flies-only water and also the start of the no-kill section. There is ample off-road parking east of the blacktop road just south of the bridge. This is also a canoe-launching site, so park well away from the landing area. James Oliver Curwood, author of many novels on the north woods, once lived on the hill south of this bridge and wrote some of his stories here.

The South Branch is 70 to 80 feet wide and 2 to 3 feet deep, with some deeper holes. Bottom is mostly gravel, with some sand and muck near the banks. The velocity is moderate, and wading is fairly easy at normal flows. The bait and spin fishermen can fish upstream from the bridge, but they must keep to the channel, as the banks upstream are private. The banks downstream are part of the Mason Tract. Upstream from the bridge the banks are generally high, and several homes overlook the river. Downstream, the banks are lower and swampy, lined with cedar, willow, and brush. Logs, snags, and overhanging brush provide good cover. Large brown trout are to be found in this water.

Site No. 2. Leline Road

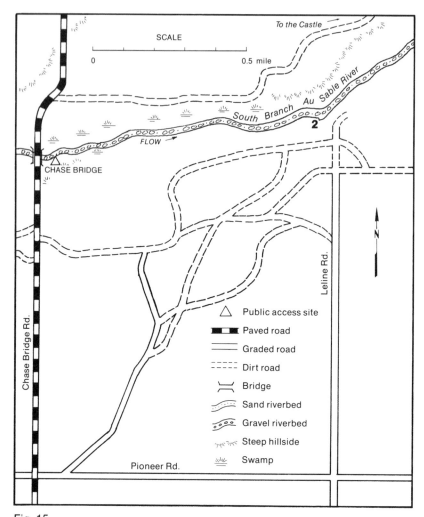

Fig. 15

Leline Road ends just south of the river near a lodge called Forest Rest. Don't try to drive down to the river, but park your car on the left (west) side of the road before you get to the steep downslope. Walk down to the end of the road and follow the path going northwest from the road to the river. The banks upstream (west) of the road are public. Downstream, the banks are private.

The river is 50 to 100 feet wide here and mostly 2 to 3 feet deep with some deeper holes. Bottom is mostly gravel with some muck and sand. Velocity generally is moderate. Wading is generally fairly easy at normal flows and the river is wide for easy fly casting. Trout cover is ample. Fishing pressure usually is light. This is part of the flies-only, no-kill water. All trout must be returned to the water.

The banks are low and covered with hardwood, conifer, and much brush.

Site No. 3. The Castle Public Access Site

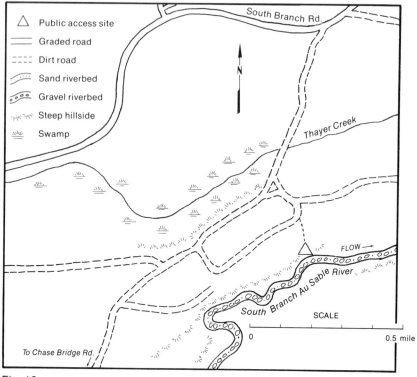

Fig. 16

When you park your car and walk down the path to the river you will pass the ruins of the old buildings before you get to the canoe landing on the left bank. If you walk more than 250 yards and still are not in sight of the river you are on the wrong path. The old foundations are all that is left of Durant's Castle, an imposing building of more than fifty rooms that was destroyed by fire in 1931, less than a year after it was completed.

The river is 60 to 80 feet wide and 3 to 5 feet deep at normal flows, with some deeper holes. Bottom is gravel, sand, clay, and boulders. The flow is fast and wading is not easy, even at normal flows. At high flows, wading is impossible. There is plenty of room to cast a fly. The left bank (the castle side) is high and sandy, with hardwood, pine, and some brush. The right bank is lower and brushier. The high banks are vulnerable to erosion, so be careful that you cause no damage when you enter or leave the stream.

You are still in the flies-only and no-kill water here. Fishing pressure usually is very light.

Site No. 4. Downey's Public Access Site

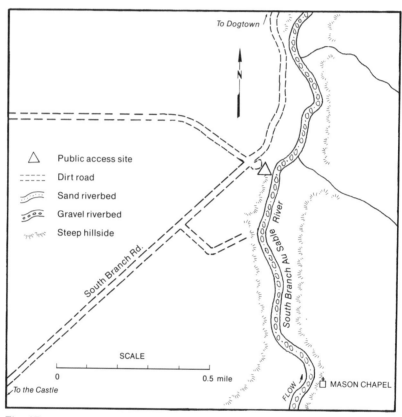

Fig. 17

You can be sure you are at Downey's when you see the stairway and stone wall along the river. Mr. Downey once owned most of the riverfront from Chase Bridge to Smith Bridge, property now included in the Mason Tract. Downey's widow sold the property to her nephew, Mr. Durant, the builder of the Castle.

The river is 70 to 90 feet wide here and 2 to 4 feet deep at normal flows, with some deeper holes. Bottom is mostly gravel and boulders, with some muck and sand along the banks. Flow is moderate to fast. It is generally easy wading here at normal flows, but difficult to impossible when the river is high. This is the place where I took a spill and broke my Fenwick flyrod, a Father's Day present from my wife.

The left bank is high and fairly open, with grass, hardwood, pine, and some brush. The right bank is low and brushy. There are remnants of an old bridge just downstream.

You are out of the no-kill water here but still restricted to flies-only. This is a popular reach of river, and heavily fished during the major hatches.

Site No. 5. Dogtown Public Access Site

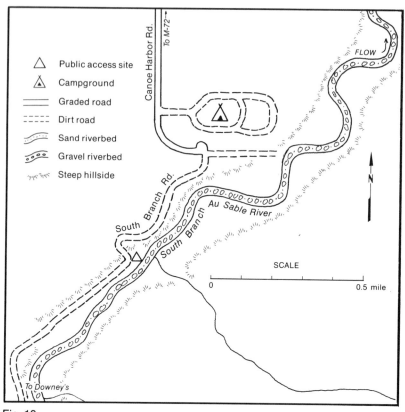

Fig. 18

This is another popular access site on the South Branch, and the parking area is closer to the river than at the Castle or Downey's.

The river is 80 to 90 feet wide and 2 to 4 feet deep at normal flows, with some deeper holes. Bottom is mostly gravel with some sand and muck. Wading is fairly easy at normal flows. Velocity is usually moderate to fast. There is plenty of room to cast a fly. Trout cover is plentiful.

The riverbanks on both sides are alternately high and low, forested with hardwoods, conifers, and much brush. This is part of the Mason Tract and is flies-only water. Fishing pressure is moderate to heavy. There are more but generally smaller trout found in this area.

Site No. 6. Canoe Harbor State Forest Campground

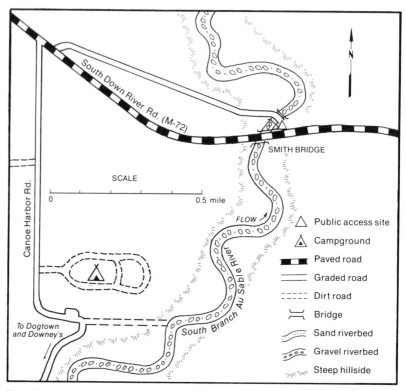

Fig. 19

In years past, the Canoe Harbor Campground was located on the river southeast of its present site. It was a pleasant campground, much used and appreciated by trout fishermen, but some of the campers (probably not trout fishermen) carelessly tramped the banks, shoving great loads of silt and sand into the river, cut saplings from the river's edge to use as tent stakes and roasting sticks for hot dogs and marshmallows, and littered the banks and their campsites with aluminum foil, bottles, and cans.

To help protect the river from further degradation the DNR moved the car-camping area to the northwest, away from the river. A group-camping area is still maintained at the old site near the river for hikers and canoeists.

If you camp at the car-camping area you can reach the river by hiking down the service road leading southeast from the east end of the camp about 450 yards to the old canoe landing. If you are not a camper you can park your car at the roadblock just south of the car campground and walk down the old road going east to the landing (see fig. 19).

The river is 60 to 80 feet wide here and 2 to 4 feet deep, with some deeper holes. Bottom is mostly gravel, with some sand and muck. Velocity is moderate to fast. The river can be waded with caution at normal flows but is unwadable at high water in early spring and after heavy rains. Fish cover is only fair on the left bank, a little better on the right. The banks are alternately high and low, forested with conifer and hardwood and some brush along the river's edge.

This part of the river seems less popular with fishermen than in years past, possibly because of intensive use by campers and canoeists. In warm weather it is not uncommon to see a bevy of bathers splashing about in the river here, an activity most discouraging to trout fishermen. However, in early morning or late evening the fishermen usually can have the river to themselves.

Site No. 7. Smith Bridge Public Access Site

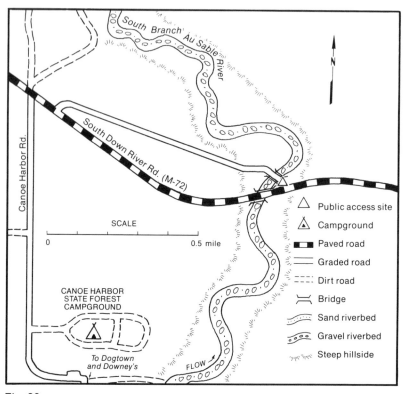

Fig. 20

This is the take-out point for most of the canoes floating the South Branch. Park your car well away from the canoe landing area. To avoid most of the canoes you need only to wade downstream a few hundred feet.

The river is 80 to 90 feet wide and mostly 2 to 4 feet deep with some deeper holes. Bottom is gravel and boulders with a little sand and muck. Velocity is moderate to fast, but at normal flows wading is fairly easy. At high flows, wading is difficult to impossible. Wading under the bridges is difficult even at normal flows. Trout cover is fair upstream, better downstream. Banks are alternately high and low, forested with conifer and hardwood, mostly pine and birch, and some brush at streamside. In spite of the intense use by canoeists and anglers in this area, there are many large brown trout here.

North Branch of the
Au Sable

Although not so famous as the Au Sable mainstream, the North Branch is a top-quality stream for brook and brown trout. It is not so heavily fished as the mainstream and has practically no canoe traffic, so you have a better chance of fishing alone here. Much of the river frontage north of Lovells is state land, and there is ample public access here. Downstream (south) from Lovells there is relatively little public land, and access is limited.

The North Branch begins as an overflow from Otsego Lake in southern Otsego County and flows generally southeastward to the north Crawford County line. Here it turns south to the village of Lovells, thence south and southeast to enter the mainstream about a mile below McMasters Bridge. Because it drains several lakes in the headwaters, the upper North Branch is too warm in summer for ideal trout water, but inflow of groundwater cools the stream so that it supports a good population of trout before it turns south into Crawford County. That part of the North Branch in Otsego County just upstream from the Crawford County line is excellent trout water, but the banks are private property. Anglers can reach this water only by wading or canoeing from public lands above or below the private holdings. It is possible, however, that the state may acquire some of this property in the near future.

From the north line of Crawford County all the way to the junction with the mainstream the North Branch provides good fishing, but that part of the river upstream from Lovells (about 5 river miles) is the favorite of many anglers. The state owns much of the frontage upstream from Twin Bridge and has recently acquired property between Twin Bridge and Lovells Bridge. The flies-only water of the North Branch begins at the Sheep Ranch Public Access

Site above Twin Bridge and continues downstream about 21 river miles to the mouth. Much of the river in Otsego County and all the river in Crawford County is wide enough for fly casting, but some parts are too deep to wade. The North Branch in the Lovells area has been dubbed "old man's fishing," because it is mostly only knee deep and easy wading, but there are holes both upstream and down that will overtop your waders.

The width of the North Branch is much more variable than that of the mainstream or South Branch. From its confluence with Chub Creek in southern Otsego County all the way to the mouth it varies in width from about 40 to more than 150 feet. The changes in width can be quite abrupt and should be a warning to wading fishermen. When the stream narrows the depth or velocity, or both, must increase, and wading will be more difficult, and, in places, impossible.

The North Branch of the Au Sable at Pipe Springs Public Access Site

The National Guard Artillery Range borders the upper North Branch on the south in Otsego County and on the west in Crawford County. For obvious reasons, fishermen should avoid crossing over into the military reservation.

The North Branch can be canoed from the Pipe Springs Public Access Site near the north Crawford County line all the way to the mouth, but not many canoeists care to make the trip. There are logjams and in-stream structures to avoid, and gravel riffles and sandy shoals to pull through at low water. Canoe liveries are reluctant to use the North Branch because the canoes do not hold up well when manned by inexperienced boaters in this water.

The North Branch was considered even better than the main-stream for brook trout in the late 1800s, according to William B. Mershon (1923). The railroad had been extended from Grayling through Lovells, and this little village became famous as a center for trout fishermen. The North Branch is still a top-notch brookie stream today, although the catches are nothing like those of the old days. There are fewer browns than brookies in the upper North Branch, but the browns run to larger size. Populations of brook trout in the North Branch above Kelloggs Bridge varied widely during the years 1975 through 1992 but were generally much higher than those of the Holy Water of the mainstream.

The summer water temperatures on the upper North Branch occasionally go as high as 80 degrees F, higher than on the flies-only section of the mainstream and much higher than the optimum for brook trout. It is probable that the trout protect themselves from the high temperatures by seeking out the colder areas where large amounts of groundwater enter the stream. One hot August afternoon I came across a brown trout of almost unbelievable size hugging the bank just above the Pipe Springs Public Access Site. When he scooted into deeper water I saw that he had been holding in a spot where a large spring entered the river. Large schools of brook trout also can be seen in springs areas in late summer.

The flow of the North Branch is remarkably stable, somewhat more stable than the mainstream and much more stable than the South Branch. Wading conditions do not change as drastically on the North Branch as on the South Branch, but caution is still advised when wading the deeper reaches. Because of the warmer water, fly hatches may occur earlier on the North Branch than on the mainstream or South Branch.

Accommodations

Fishermen can find lodging in many motels and cabins in Gaylord and Grayling, and there are excellent restaurants in these cities. Good food can also be obtained in the little village of Lovells. Streamside accommodations on the North Branch are meager, but there are a few rental cabins in the Lovells area, and camping is permitted on state lands in two of the public access sites on the river. Although not on the river, Shupac Lake State Forest Campground north of Lovells is a convenient headquarters for fishermen on the upper North Branch. This campground has spaces for thirty camping parties and is equipped with water supply, picnic tables, and outdoor toilets. More modern facilities are available at Otsego Lake State Park south of Gaylord.

Fishing tackle of all kinds can be bought in Grayling and Gaylord, and good trout flies are also available in Lovells.

Maps of the North Branch

The stream channel and public roads leading to the North Branch in Crawford County are shown on the location map (fig. 21). It is well to remember that the roads and trails in the military reservation south and west of the river are not open to the public.

The Pipe Springs Public Access Site (site 1, fig. 22) is exactly 0.5 mile south of the north Crawford County line. Starting at the bridge on County 612 in Lovells, go west about 0.2 mile to the intersection with Twin Bridge Road taking off to the right (northwest). Go northwest and north on Twin Bridge Road. You will cross Twin Bridge about 1.6 miles north of the intersection. Continue on north. About 1 mile north of Twin Bridge the road swings to the right (east) and then to the left (north) again. About 1.7 miles beyond the bridge you will come to an inconspicuous dirt road leading off to the left (west). Turn left on this road and go about 0.1 mile to the river.

The Sheep Ranch Public Access Site (site 2, fig. 23) is about 0.5 mile north of Twin Bridge, or about 2.1 miles north of the intersection of Twin Bridge Road and County 612.

Twin Bridge (site 3, fig. 24) is about 1.6 miles north of the intersection of Twin Bridge Road with County 612.

Lovells Bridge (site 4, fig. 25) is in the village of Lovells on

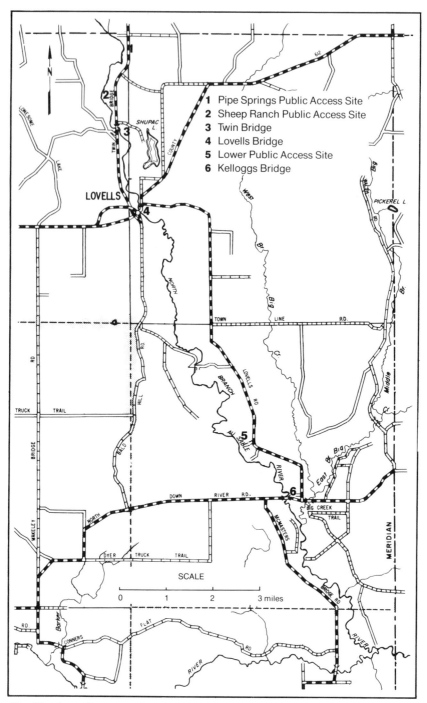

1 Pipe Springs Public Access Site
2 Sheep Ranch Public Access Site
3 Twin Bridge
4 Lovells Bridge
5 Lower Public Access Site
6 Kelloggs Bridge

Fig. 21. Location map of the North Branch Au Sable

County 612. To get to Lovells go north out of Grayling on Old U.S. 27 about 2.5 miles to the intersection with Hartwick Pines Road. Turn right (northeast) on this road and go about 8 miles to the intersection with County 612. Turn right (east) on County 612 and go about 9 miles to the village of Lovells.

You can get to the Lower Public Access Site (site 5, fig. 26) by driving east and then south out of Lovells on Lovells Road about 6.5 miles to a dirt road turning off to the right (west). Follow this winding road about 0.5 mile to the river. This public access site can also be reached from the south. Starting at Kelloggs Bridge on the North Down River Road, about 18 miles east of Grayling, go east on the North Down River Road about 0.3 mile to the intersection with Lovells Road. Turn left (north) on this blacktop road and go about 1.6 miles to a dirt road leading off to the left (west). Lovells Road makes a bend to the right (north) just before the turnoff. Follow the dirt road generally westward about 0.5 mile to the river.

Kelloggs Bridge (site 6, fig. 27) is on the North Down River Road about 18 miles east of Grayling.

Site No. 1. Pipe Springs Public Access Site

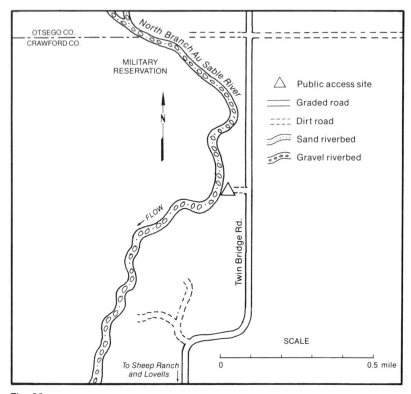

Fig. 22

Camping is permitted at this site, and most of the campers are fishermen. Two horizontal pipes tap springs on the east (left) bank for water supply. I do not know if these springs have been tested for purity, but I have drunk from them many times in the past twenty years without apparent ill effects. Outdoor toilets are also provided. There are no designated camping spaces here, but it is wise to camp some distance from the river to protect the banks and to keep out of the way of fishermen going to and from the river.

The width of the North Branch varies considerably here. Downstream from the access site it is 70 to 90 feet wide and 2 to 3 feet deep with some deeper holes. Upstream it is 50 to 70 feet wide and 2 to 4 feet deep with some holes that will overtop your waders. Bottom is gravel and sand with some muck. The stream velocity is slow to moderate in the wider areas and moderate to fast where the stream narrows. Wading downstream is fairly easy if you watch out for the deeper holes. Upstream, wading is more difficult, and there is some water that cannot be waded. The stream is wide and open enough for all kinds of fishing. Trout cover, some of it man-made, is adequate. There is a good population of large brown trout in this part of the North Branch.

There are no special regulations for this water at present, and spin and bait fishermen have good success here, especially in the deeper waters upstream. Early season fly hatches are good on this water, sometimes better than on the mainstream. Fishing pressure usually is moderate.

Site No. 2. Sheep Ranch Public Access Site

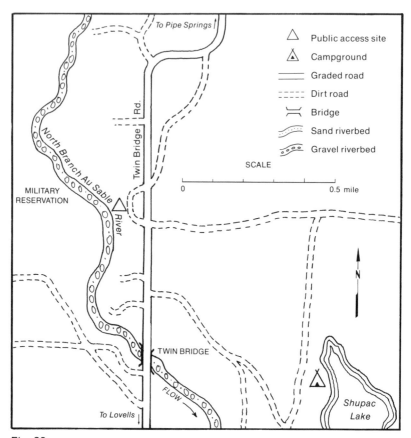

Fig. 23

The Sheep Ranch is a large open grassland area with some scrub jack pine and poplar. There is ample room to park your car and walk down one of the paths to the river. There is a sign at streamside marking the exact boundary between the standard-regulation water upstream and the flies-only special-regulation water downstream. The riverbanks, both sides, are state land at the access site and upstream. Downstream from the access site, both banks are private.

The river is 50 to 100 feet wide and 2 to 3 feet deep, with a few deeper holes. Bottom is gravel with some sand and muck and a few boulders. Velocity of flow is slow to moderate. Wading is easy, and there is room enough to cast a fly. The banks are low and brushy. Fish cover is very good. This is a pleasant reach to fish, and you may often have the river to yourself here. Fly-fishermen usually stick to the flies-only water, leaving the river upstream to the bait and spin fishermen.

Site No. 3. Twin Bridge

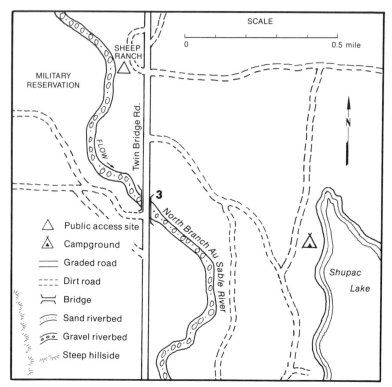

SCALE

0   0.5 mile

SHEEP RANCH

MILITARY RESERVATION

Twin Bridge Rd.

FLOW

3

North Branch Au Sable River

Shupac Lake

△ Public access site
△ Campground
═ Graded road
--- Dirt road
⋈ Bridge
Sand riverbed
Gravel riverbed
Steep hillside

N

Fig. 24

The road shoulder is not too wide near the bridge, but there is just enough room to park two or three cars on the east side of the road south of the bridge. Be sure you are out of the traffic lane. There is a wider shoulder and better parking about one-fourth mile north of the bridge.

The North Branch is 100 to 125 feet wide here and 1 to 3 feet deep, with a few deeper holes. Bottom is gravel, sand, and some muck. Velocity is slow to moderate and wading is easy. The river is wide and open for easy fly-fishing. Trout cover is good. The banks average about 4 feet high, are brushy, and are lined with hardwoods and a few conifers and small grassy areas. Fishing pressure usually is moderate.

This is all private land, except for the road right-of-way, and there are several homes and cabins on the river. You will have to stick to the channel, fishing upstream or down.

Site No. 4. Lovells Bridge

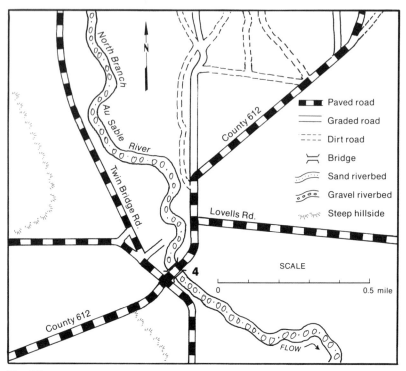

Fig. 25

There is room to park three or four cars on the downstream side (southeast) of the road just northeast of the bridge.

The river is 60 to 100 feet wide here and 2 to 3 feet deep, with some deeper holes. Bottom is mostly gravel, with some sand and muck. The velocity generally is moderate and wading is fairly easy. The right bank is high and steep, the left bank lower and brushy. The land is all private except for the road right-of-way. Trout cover is somewhat sparse. Fishing pressure usually is moderate.

Site No. 5. Lower Public Access Site

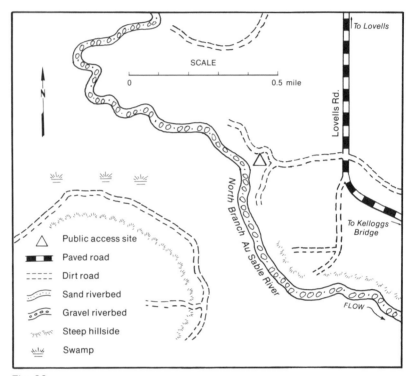

SCALE

0   0.5 mile

N

To Lovells

Lovells Rd.

North Branch Au Sable River

To Kelloggs
Bridge

FLOW

△   Public access site
▪▪▪▫▪   Paved road
------   Dirt road
∿∿∿   Sand riverbed
∘∘∘∘   Gravel riverbed
⋎⋏⋎   Steep hillside
⋇⋇   Swamp

Fig. 26

This public access site, known as the Lower Public Access Site, is the only developed access on the lower North Branch. There is a large acreage of state land here with more than a half-mile of public frontage on both banks. Camping is permitted, but there are no designated camp spaces. Outdoor toilets are provided.

When you turn west off Lovells Road you will shortly come to a large open area with a scattering of small trees. The rough dirt road winds around through this open area and comes to a fork before you reach the river. Either fork leads to places where you can park your car and walk down to the stream.

The river is extremely variable in width here, ranging from about 40 to more than 100 feet. Depth also is quite variable, from about 2 to more than 4 feet. Bottom is gravel, sand, and muck. The stream flows fast here, and wading is difficult in some of the deeper, narrower parts and impossible in others. Be especially careful around wing dams and other in-stream obstacles. Fly casting is not so easy as in other parts of the river because you must wade near the banks in many places especially in the upstream reaches. This part of the river usually is not heavily fished.

The stream banks are low and brushy, with some hardwood and cedar.

Site No. 6. Kelloggs Bridge

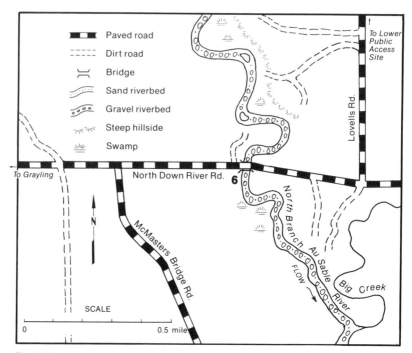

Fig. 27

There is room to park three or four cars on the north side of the road just east of the bridge.

The river is 60 to 100 feet wide and mostly 2 to 4 feet deep, with some parts over your wader tops. Bottom is mostly gravel, with some sand and muck. The flow is fast and wading is not easy. At high water, wading may be impossible. The river is open and wide enough for fly casting. The banks are low, forested with mixed pine and hardwood and some brush. Trout cover is somewhat sparse. Fishing pressure usually is light. Except for the road right-of-way, this is all private land. Some large brown trout are in this part of the North Branch.

Manistee River

The Manistee River, like its sister stream, the Au Sable, is one of Michigan's classic trout streams. Although not so famous as the Au Sable, the Manistee provides excellent fishing to those who know it. Upstream from Cameron Bridge the river is rated as a first-class trout stream by the DNR. Downstream, it is rated fair to good. Because of the lighter fishing pressure, angler success appears to be as good on the Manistee as on its more famous sister. Aesthetically, the Manistee is one of Michigan's most attractive rivers. Its waters flow cool and clean, and its banks are forested with pine, cedar, spruce, poplar, maple, and oak. In the fall, the brilliant warm colors of the hardwoods are pleasingly contrasted with the deep greens of the conifers. The Manistee has never had the cabin development nor the intensive fishing pressure of the Au Sable, and the upper reaches have more of a wilderness atmosphere than most of the upper Au Sable.

Although early French explorers called the Au Sable "the river of sands," the upper Manistee is far sandier than the Au Sable. The sandy streambed with very little gravel for spawning probably accounts for the lower trout productivity on the Manistee. Except for the limited spawning beds, the Manistee is ideal trout water. The flow is remarkably stable, more stable than even the Au Sable, and the summer water temperatures are cooler than those of the Au Sable.

Like the Au Sable, the Manistee was famous for its grayling fishing before it became known as a trout stream. Thadeus Norris (*Scribners Monthly* 1879) told of catching grayling in great numbers in both the Au Sable and the Manistee in the late 1870s. According to some old-time residents of Grayling, the Manistee was still producing good catches of grayling after the fish had become scarce in the Au Sable. The late P. W. Christenson told me he caught sixty-five grayling on the Manistee in one day in 1899. The fish were to be kept alive for display at an exposition, but half the grayling died overnight, and the rest were returned to the river.

The Manistee rises in the sandy glacial deposits in southeastern Antrim County. Its headwaters are only a few miles west of those of the Au Sable, and the two streams flow southward in generally parallel courses for about 15 miles. Here the streams part company, the Au Sable turning east to Lake Huron while the Manistee turns west to Lake Michigan.

This guide includes the upper river from Deward downstream to Sharon, about 40 river miles. This part of the river is considered best for resident trout. The lower river is best known for steelhead and salmon fishing.

From the deserted village of Deward downstream to Cameron Bridge, about 4 river miles, the Manistee is 30 to 50 feet wide and mostly 2 to 4 feet deep with some deeper runs. Bottom is sand and

The Manistee River near M-72 Bridge

gravel. The banks are mostly low and brushy, forested with hard-wood, with some higher banks and open grassland near Deward. This part of the river has adequate spawning beds and is considered by many to offer the best fishing for resident trout on the Manistee. However, large brown trout are found at all sites on the Manistee.

From Cameron Bridge downstream to about a mile above the M-72 Bridge, about 10 river miles, the Manistee is almost all sand bottom, with a few small patches of gravel. The banks are alternately coniferous swamp and pine upland. The river is mostly 2 to 4 feet deep, with some parts over your wader tops and a few holes over your head. Below Cameron Bridge and again below Red Bridge the river splits into several narrow channels less than 3 feet deep. These can cause some confusion to the canoeist, but if you stick to the channel carrying the most water you should come out all right. Unlike the Pigeon and Black north of Gaylord, few of the channels come to a dead end. Although not rated as top-quality trout water, this part of the river provides good fishing to many anglers. The Upper Manistee River State Forest Campground is located on the right bank of the Manistee downstream from Red Bridge.

As you approach the M-72 Bridge (going downstream) the bottom becomes more gravelly, and gravel bottom predominates from here to about 2 river miles below the bridge. From this point downstream to about 1 mile above Sharon (about 22 river miles) the bottom is mostly sand again, although there are a few gravel riffles. The river is 60 to 120 feet wide and 3 to 6 feet deep in most of the 25 river miles between the M-72 Bridge and Sharon. There is wadable water near the M-72 Bridge and at Sharon and in some of the shallower reaches in between, but most of this water must be waded near the banks or not at all. The riverbanks are alternately high and low, but generally higher than upstream, forested with mostly upland pine and hardwood. The Manistee River Bridge Campground is just upstream from the M-72 Bridge, and another campground is at the CCC Bridge. The only flies-only water on the Manistee extends from the CCC Campground upstream 7.5 river miles.

Upstream from the M-72 Bridge much of the river frontage is in state lands and public access is plentiful. Downstream from M-72 all the way to Sharon almost all the frontage is private and public access is very limited. This part of the river is best fished by boat.

Accommodations

The town of Grayling probably is the best headquarters for fishing the upper Manistee, and Kalkaska is convenient for fishing the Sharon area. There is a wide variety of motels and restaurants in both these towns. Good food can also be obtained in the little village of Frederic, about 8 miles north of Grayling. Fishing tackle of all kinds can be purchased in Grayling, Kalkaska, and Frederic, and in other small stores along M-72 west of Grayling.

Canoes and pickup service are supplied by liveries in Grayling and on the river. Guide service, including Au Sable Riverboats, is available in Grayling.

Three state forest campgrounds are on the upper river. The Upper Manistee River Campground west of Frederic has spaces for thirty camping parties. The Manistee River Bridge Campground west of Grayling has twenty-three spaces, and the CCC Bridge Campground near Sharon also has twenty-three spaces. Spaces usually are available at one or more of these campgrounds except during the holiday weekends.

Maps of the Manistee

The channel of the Manistee and public roads leading to the river are shown on the location maps (figs. 28 and 29). The access sites on these maps are numbered in downstream order, starting with site 1 at Deward and ending with site 8 at Sharon.

The village of Frederic is about 8 miles north of Grayling on Old U.S. 27. This is a convenient starting point for the first four access sites. To get to Deward (site 1, fig. 30) go west out of Frederic on the blacktop County 612 about 0.5 mile, then turn right (north) on Kolka Creek Road about 1.3 miles to the intersection with Cameron Bridge Road leading off to the left (west). Turn left on this road and go about 1 mile to the intersection with Deward Road leading off to the right (north). Turn right on Deward Road and follow this road, first north about 2.1 miles, then west about 1 mile, then north, northwest, and finally southwest about 1.5 miles to the Deward area. Nothing remains of the old village, but there are signs posted by the DNR giving rules for the use of the Deward area.

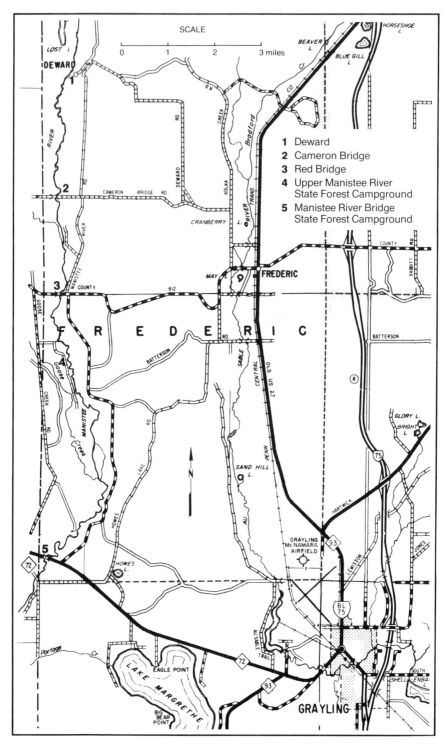

1 Deward
2 Cameron Bridge
3 Red Bridge
4 Upper Manistee River
  State Forest Campground
5 Manistee River Bridge
  State Forest Campground

Fig. 28.   Location map of the Manistee, Deward to M-72

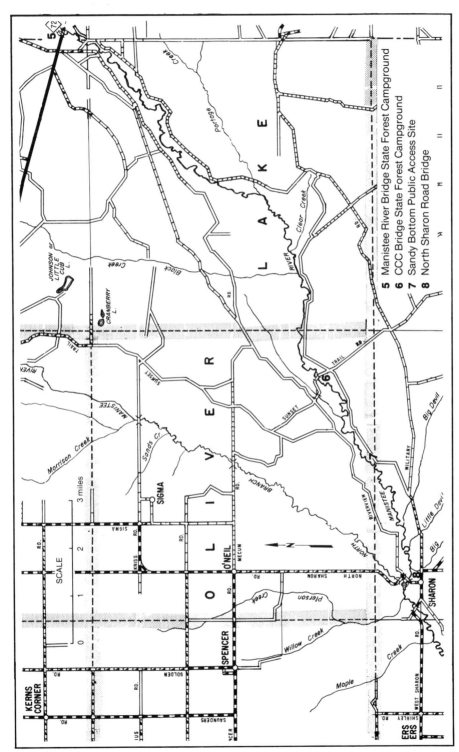

5   Manistee River Bridge State Forest Campground
6   CCC Bridge State Forest Campground
7   Sandy Bottom Public Access Site
8   North Sharon Road Bridge

Fig. 29.   Location map of the Manistee: M 72 to Sharon

Cameron Bridge (site 2, fig. 31) is about 2.5 miles south of Deward. Go west out of Frederic on County 612 about 0.5 mile, then turn right (north) on Kolka Creek Road and go about 1.3 miles to the intersection with Cameron Bridge Road. Turn left (west) on Cameron Bridge Road and continue west about 3.7 miles to the bridge. To get to Cameron Bridge from Deward, go south about 2.6 miles on Manistee River Road to Cameron Bridge Road, then turn right (west) on Cameron Bridge Road and go about 0.5 mile to the bridge.

Red Bridge (site 3, fig. 32), also called 612 Bridge, is 2 miles south of Cameron Bridge. Go west out of Frederic on County 612 and follow this road about 5.3 miles to the bridge. To get to Red Bridge from Cameron Bridge, go east from Cameron Bridge on Cameron Bridge Road about 0.5 mile to the intersection with Manistee River Road. Turn right (south) on this road and go about 2.1 miles to County 612. Turn right (west) on 612 and go 0.1 mile to the bridge.

Upper Manistee River Campground (site 4, fig. 33) is about 1.5 miles south of Red Bridge on the right (west) bank of the river. Go west from Red Bridge on County 612 about 0.6 mile to the intersection with Goose Creek Road. Turn left (south) on this dirt road and go about 1 mile to the intersection with another dirt road leading off to the left (east). There is a DNR sign at this intersection marked "Upper Manistee River State Forest Campground." Turn left here and follow this road east and south about 0.9 mile to the campground.

Manistee River Bridge Campground (site 5, fig. 34) is on the right (west) bank of the river just upstream from the M-72 Bridge. Go west out of Grayling on M-72 about 8 miles to the bridge. Cross the bridge and turn right (north) into the campground.

The CCC Bridge Campground (site 6, fig. 35) is on the Manistee about 10 miles southwest (downstream) from the M-72 Bridge. Go west on M-72 from the bridge about 6.7 miles to the intersection with Sunset Trail Road. Turn left (south) on Sunset Trail Road and follow this road generally south about 8 miles to the CCC Bridge. There are several other dirt roads leading off from Sunset Trail Road, but if you keep to the main-traveled road and keep heading generally south you should have no trouble. The campground is on both sides of the river right at the bridge.

To get to the CCC Bridge Campground from Sharon, go east

out of Sharon on Military Road about 1.8 miles to a Y intersection. There is a sign marked "Manistee River" on the left fork. Take this (left) fork and go generally northeast about 3.4 miles to the intersection with Sunset Trail Road. Turn left (north) on Sunset Trail and go about 0.3 mile to the CCC Bridge.

Site 7 (fig. 36) is a public access site about 2.5 miles northeast of Sharon. Go east out of Sharon on Military Road about 1.8 miles to the Y intersection described above. Again, take the left fork and go about 1.2 miles to the access site on the left (northwest) side of the road. The road runs very close to the river here.

Site 8 (fig. 37) is the bridge on North Sharon Road. The bridge is about 0.3 mile north of the intersection of North Sharon Road with West Sharon Road.

Site No. 1. Deward

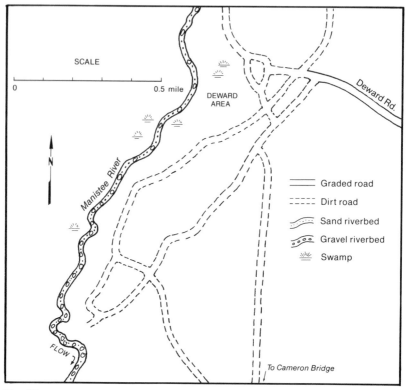

Fig. 30

When you drive into the Deward area you will see signs posted by the DNR marked "Deward Area. Motorized use prohibited except on roads signed as being open." None of the roads close to the stream are open to cars, but you can park off the road at several places and walk down the roads or across the fields a few hundred yards to the river. Camping is permitted here, but you must keep within 50 feet of a road open to motorized vehicles. In other words, you cannot camp on or near the stream banks.

The Manistee is 30 to 40 feet wide and mostly less than 3 feet deep. About a mile downstream from the deserted village the river deepens, and some holes and runs may overtop your waders. The bottom is mostly sand with scattered patches of gravel, but gravel becomes more abundant downstream. Banks upstream are mostly low and mucky; downstream, the banks are high and sandy.

This is a pleasant place to fish, and there are large brown trout here. The open grassland on the left (east) bank makes it possible to fish from the banks, and the bait fisherman can drift his worm through the deeper runs without spooking the trout. The fly-fisherman, too, can cast from the banks in places, or wade the shallower parts with ease. The generally open water makes fly-fishing relatively easy for such a narrow stream.

There is a lot of water that can be fished here without trespassing on private property. State-owned lands include the stream banks on both sides of the river for about 1 mile upstream and 2 miles downstream from Deward.

Site No. 2. Cameron Bridge

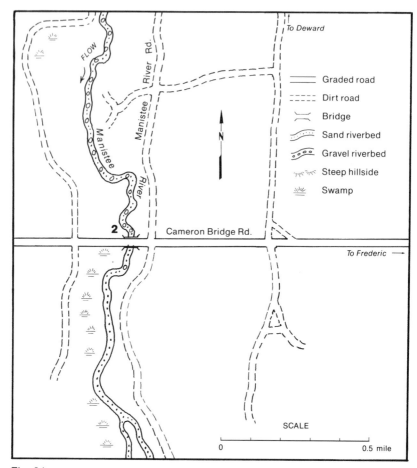

Graded road
Dirt road
Bridge
Sand riverbed
Gravel riverbed
Steep hillside
Swamp

To Deward
Manistee River Rd.
FLOW
Manistee River
Cameron Bridge Rd.
To Frederic
N
SCALE
0   0.5 mile
2

Fig. 31

There is just room to park one or two cars on the north side of the road west of the bridge. The river here is 40 to 50 feet wide. Upstream, it is generally less than 4 feet deep, with some deeper holes. At the bridge and downstream, it is mostly more than 4 feet deep at mid-channel. Bottom is sand and gravel upstream, mostly sand downstream. Velocity is moderate. There is a high, sandy bank on the east side of the river downstream from the bridge. Otherwise the banks are low, sandy or mucky, forested with conifer and hardwood. There are some brushy banks, especially upstream from the bridge. Except for the road right-of-way, the banks are private property, upstream and down.

The river can be waded most places upstream from the bridge. Downstream, it is wadable in parts, but it is mostly too deep at mid-channel for easy wading. The river is open and wide enough for fly-fishing and deep enough for spin and bait fishing. Although considered one of the best spots on the Manistee for resident trout, the river here is not usually heavily fished. One of the largest brown trout taken on a fly in Michigan (15 pounds, 2 ounces) was caught in this area.

Site No. 3. Red Bridge

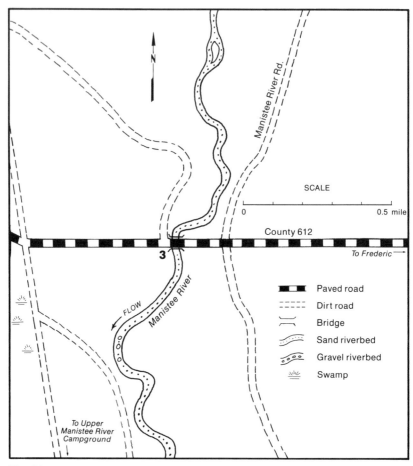

Fig. 32

There is room to park two or three cars on either side of County 612 east of the bridge. Be careful in walking down the road embankment that you do not damage the vegetation and start erosion. This is all private property at the bridge and upstream. There is some state land downstream.

The Manistee is 60 to 80 feet wide here and generally more than 3 feet deep at mid-channel. It can be waded with caution in places, but there are holes that will overtop your waders. Velocity of flow is moderate. The bottom is mostly sand, soft and shifting in places, and the footing for the wading fisherman is not always the best. The banks at the bridge and downstream are high and sandy, with pine forest and some open grassland. Upstream, the banks are coniferous swamp.

The river here is wide enough for easy fly casting and deep enough for all kinds of fishing, including bait and spin fishing. Fishing pressure usually is moderate.

Site No. 4. Upper Manistee River
State Forest Campground

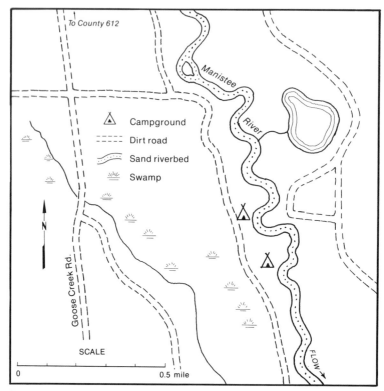

To County 612

Manistee

River

△ Campground

- - - - Dirt road

Sand riverbed

Swamp

N

Goose Creek Rd.

SCALE

0   0.5 mile

FLOW

Fig. 33

There are two camping areas here, one for car camping and one for group canoe camping. This is an attractive campground, with mature red pine, oak, and maple. The river is about 50 feet wide and mostly less than 4 feet deep at mid-channel. However, there are some deeper holes, and at least one of these is over your head. The bottom is almost entirely sand, soft and shifting in places. The river divides into more than one channel in places. Banks are alternately high and sandy and low and mucky, forested with conifer. The river is wide enough for easy fly casting and shallow enough to wade if you watch out for the deeper holes and shifting sands. Fishing pressure usually is light.

The riverbanks at the campground and for about a half-mile downstream are state land. Upstream, part of the riverfrontage is private.

Site No. 5. Manistee River Bridge State Forest Campground

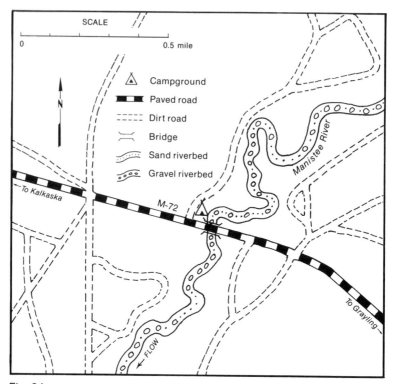

SCALE

0   0.5 mile

N

△ Campground

▬ Paved road

----- Dirt road

⌒ Bridge

〜 Sand riverbed

∘∘∘ Gravel riverbed

To Kalkaska

M-72

Manistee River

To Grayling

FLOW

Fig. 34

This is one of the few state forest campgrounds where the campsites have not been moved back away from the river. It is too close to M-72 and developed areas to give any sort of wilderness atmosphere, but it is a convenient spot from which to fish this part of the Manistee. All camping spaces may be filled on summer weekends, but few of the campers fish the river here.

The river here is 80 to 90 feet wide and 2 to 4 feet deep with some deeper holes. Bottom is mostly gravel. Banks are high and sandy, forested with pine and some oak. The river is wide and open enough for easy fly-fishing. Wading is fairly easy if you watch out for the deeper holes. Many canoes float the water here, but fishing pressure usually is light. Except for the campground on the west bank, the riverfrontage is all private.

Site No. 6. CCC Bridge State Forest Campground

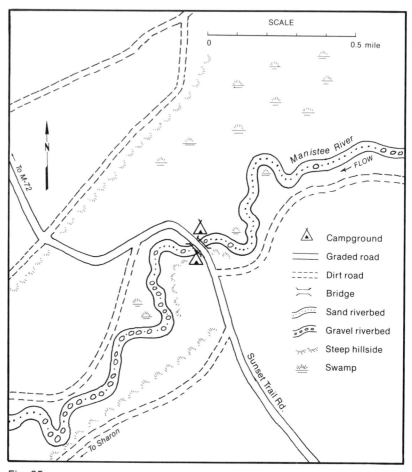

SCALE

0   0.5 mile

Manistee River

← FLOW

To M-72

To Sharon

Sunset Trail Rd.

△ Campground
━━ Graded road
╌╌╌╌ Dirt road
⌣ Bridge
⌒ Sand riverbed
∘∘∘ Gravel riverbed
⋎⋎ Steep hillside
≋ Swamp

Fig. 35

This campground is popular with canoeists but rarely used by fishermen. There are campsites on both sides of the river near the bridge and a canoe landing on the left (south) bank.

The Manistee is a big river here, 100 to 120 feet wide and generally more than 3 feet deep at mid-channel. Bottom is sand with a few patches of gravel. The gravel beds do not appear favorable for spawning as they are mostly choked with sand. Velocity of flow is moderate. Parts of the river here can be waded with care at normal flows if you avoid the holes, which may be more than 6 feet deep. At high flows the river is mostly unwadable. There is plenty of room to fish with fly, bait, or spinning lures, but the spin and bait fishermen must stick to the water downstream from the bridge, as the river upstream is restricted to flies-only.

The banks at the campground are high and sandy, with an open stand of pine and hardwood. Upstream and down are low, brushy banks. The banks at the campground are most vulnerable to erosion, and fishermen should be especially careful here to enter and leave the stream with the least possible disturbance.

Site No. 7. Sandy Bottom Public Access Site

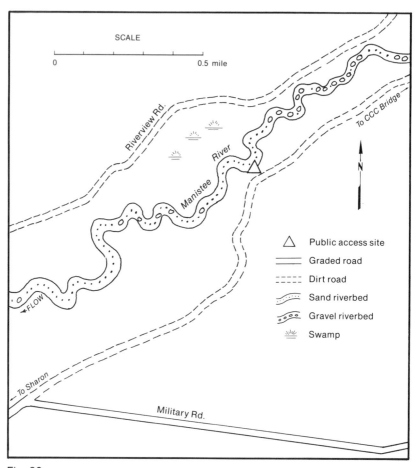

SCALE

0   0.5 mile

Riverview Rd.

Manistee River

To CCC Bridge

N

FLOW

To Sharon

Military Rd.

△ Public access site

Graded road

Dirt road

Sand riverbed

Gravel riverbed

Swamp

Fig. 36

As far as I know, this public access site has not been given a name, so I have taken the liberty of calling it "Sandy Bottom." It is the only public access to the Manistee between the CCC Campground and Sharon. There is plenty of room to park several cars here but there are no other facilities.

The river is about 120 feet wide here and 2 to 4 feet deep, with some holes downstream more than 6 feet deep. Bottom is sand. The velocity is moderate and much of the river can be waded with care at normal flows. Drowned logs and snags along the banks provide good trout cover. The south bank is 5 to 8 feet high, forested with hardwood and some large white pines. The north bank is lower, with coniferous swamp and some brush. Fishing pressure here is very light.

Site No. 8. North Sharon Road Bridge

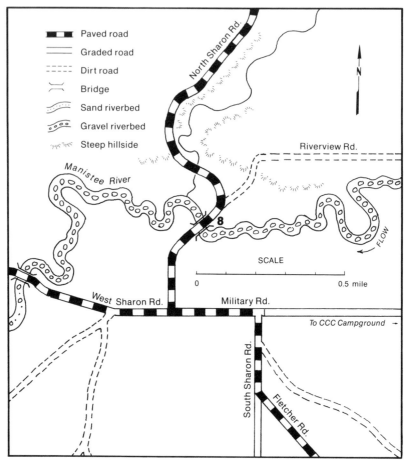

Fig. 37

There is room to park on both sides of North Sharon Road southwest of the bridge. Gravel riffles less than 3 feet deep alternate with deep pools, some more than 6 feet deep. The river is about 100 feet wide. Parts of the river can be waded with care at normal flows, but the velocity is fast, the rocks are slippery, and wading is never easy. Bottom is mostly gravel and cobbles with some sand. The banks are alternately high and sandy and low and mucky, forested with hardwood and some pine. There is some brush along the river's edge. Cover is sparse in this part of the river. Canoes are sometimes landed at this bridge. Fishing pressure is light.

Pigeon River

The Pigeon River, in the northern part of Michigan's Lower Peninsula, is an outstanding trout stream and the favorite of a select company of anglers who return here year after year. If you enjoy fishing a relatively small, friendly stream in a beautiful north-woods setting, the Pigeon could become your favorite, too. The Pigeon is best known for its excellent brook-trout fishing, but it also supports a good population of brown trout and some rainbow in the lower reaches. Much of the river flows through state land, so access sites are plentiful. Three attractive campgrounds are on the river. The Pigeon is not so heavily fished as some of the better-known Michigan streams, such as the Au Sable and Pere Marquette. A fisherman in search of solitude can find it on the Pigeon if he is willing to hike a mile or two from the roads. He should carry a map and compass to avoid getting lost on cloudy days.

The fisherman on the Pigeon is rarely bothered by canoes. The many portages required around logjams discourage all but the most enthusiastic of canoeists.

The Pigeon River rises in a cedar swamp northeast of Gaylord and flows generally northward about 43 river miles to discharge into Mullett Lake near Indian River. I-75 roughly parallels the Pigeon about 5 to 10 miles to the west. Exits from this highway at Gaylord, Vanderbilt, Wolverine, and Indian River provide access to the river.

A tiny brook in the headwaters, the Pigeon is more than 60 feet wide in places in the lower river. Forest cover is mostly coniferous swamp in the headwaters, but hardwoods are more plentiful in the lower reaches. Above Pigeon Bridge Campground most of the river frontage is private property. From Pigeon Bridge downstream to McIntosh Landing most is state land, but there are some private holdings. Downstream from McIntosh Landing most land is private.

Upstream from the Old Vanderbilt Road Bridge the Pigeon is not easy to fish, because the channel is narrow, and overhanging branches make casting difficult. These conditions discourage many fishermen, but make it all the better for those who are willing to give it a try. There is an excellent population of brook trout here eager to take your bait or fly.

From Old Vanderbilt Road Bridge downstream to Pigeon Bridge Campground the river is wider and more open, and fly casting is easier. The Song of the Morning Ranch Pond is in this reach.

Between Pigeon Bridge Campground and Pine Grove Campground there are 10 miles of river virtually unequalled in the state for superb trout fishing and unspoiled scenic beauty. The river is wide enough for all kinds of fishing, and most of it is wadable at normal flows. There is easy access to the river at several points. The farther you get from the access roads the better your chance of having the stream to yourself.

Downstream from Pine Grove Campground the Pigeon is wider and deeper, and wading is not so easy. At high flows, wading

The Pigeon River near Pigeon Bridge Campground

may be impossible. Slippery boulders and bedrock in places are an additional hazard to the wading fisherman. Trout populations generally decline as you go downstream, but the fish may run larger. Brown trout predominate over brook trout in this part of the river.

If you plan to fish the Pigeon from a boat, be prepared to lift it over or around several logjams. A boat can be useful in reaching the remote parts of the river, but you may want to tie it up and fish by wading, once you reach the desired spot. Do not try to float the lower river to the mouth at Mullett Lake. The braided channels near the mouth will cause great confusion and long portages. You will find yourself dragging the boat from one narrowing channel to another, trying to find the one that continues on to the lake.

The Pigeon was designated a Wild-Scenic River by the Michigan Natural Resources Commission in June, 1982. A stream so designated will be protected from development and activities that may damage or destroy its fish, wildlife, aesthetic, and recreational values. Few, if any, of the streams in the Lower Peninsula are more deserving of such protection.

Like the Au Sable, the Pigeon River has a large component of groundwater inflow that keeps a good flow during summer droughts and cools the water. Unlike the Au Sable, however, the Pigeon also gets a large amount of surface runoff from the steep morainal hills with less permeable soils just north of Gaylord. For this reason the Pigeon rises faster and higher than the Au Sable after heavy spring rains and snowmelt. The average annual range in stage on the Pigeon near Vanderbilt is 3.3 feet, whereas the Au Sable rarely rises more than 1 foot.

Summer water temperatures on the Pigeon run a little higher than the optimum for trout. The maximum summer temperatures generally increase downstream, where groundwater inflow is not so great. Like all the trout streams in the northern part of the Lower Peninsula, the water is hard and slightly alkaline, not likely to be affected by acid rains.

The organic silt that entered the Pigeon from the Song of the Morning Ranch Pond in 1984 reduced trout populations in some of the access sites. The sites most affected were Pigeon Bridge and Pigeon River campgrounds (sites 3 and 4). Sites 1 and 2 are upstream from the pond and were not affected. The Pigeon has recovered from the results of this accident.

The Pigeon got its name from the passenger pigeon, which formerly thrived in the hardwood forests of Michigan. The river has been known as a top-quality trout stream for nearly a century, and continues to hold that reputation to this day. Much of our understanding of the trout's response to changes in environment comes from research at the Pigeon River Trout Research Station near Vanderbilt. In recent years oil and gas development in the Pigeon River country has detracted from the wilderness atmosphere of the area, but the development so far has been to the south and east of the river itself. Trout fishermen hope the designation of the Pigeon as a Wild-Scenic River will help protect it from future degradation.

Accommodations

Gaylord and Indian River have a wide variety of motels and restaurants to serve you. More limited but adequate accommodations can also be found in the smaller towns of Vanderbilt and Wolverine.

For those who want to camp there are three state forest campgrounds on the Pigeon. These provide tent and trailer campers with designated campsites, water supply, picnic tables, and toilets.

Fishing tackle of all kinds can be purchased in Gaylord and Indian River. Stores in Vanderbilt and Wolverine also carry some tackle.

Maps of the Pigeon

The stream channel and all public roads leading to the Pigeon are shown on the location map (fig. 38). Eight numbered access sites are shown on this map. For each of these eight sites are larger-scale maps showing the river channel in greater detail.

There are many routes that will get you to the Pigeon from Gaylord, Vanderbilt, Wolverine, and Indian River, but some of these may be hard to follow if you are not familiar with the area. Probably the easiest way is to take the Sturgeon Valley Road east out of Vanderbilt and follow this all the way to the Pigeon Bridge Campground (about 10 miles). Turn left (north) into the campground just past (east of) the bridge. Although the campground is called the Pigeon Bridge Campground, the bridge itself is sometimes referred to as the Sturgeon Valley Road Bridge.

The Pigeon Bridge Campground is site 3 (fig. 41) on your

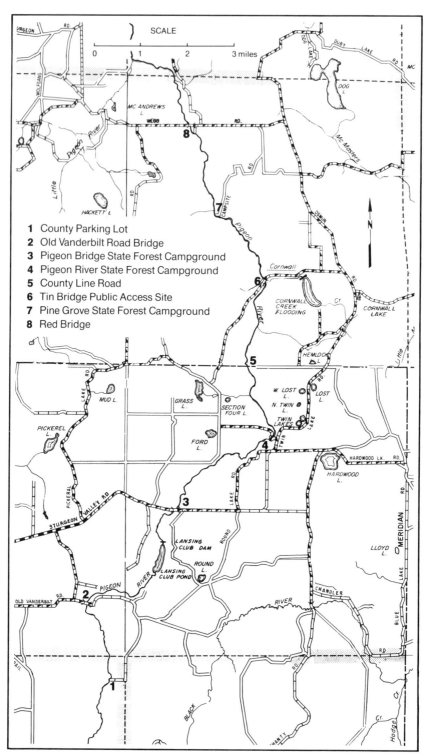

1 County Parking Lot
2 Old Vanderbilt Road Bridge
3 Pigeon Bridge State Forest Campground
4 Pigeon River State Forest Campground
5 County Line Road
6 Tin Bridge Public Access Site
7 Pine Grove State Forest Campground
8 Red Bridge

Fig. 38.   Location map of the Pigeon River

map. Use this as the starting point for the other sites. To get to Old Vanderbilt Road Bridge (site 2, fig. 40), go back west from the bridge on Sturgeon Valley Road (toward Vanderbilt) about 3 miles to a gravel road leading off to the left (south). Take this road south about 1.5 miles to the intersection with Old Vanderbilt Road. Turn left again (east) on Old Vanderbilt Road and go about 0.3 mile to the bridge.

The County Parking Lot (site 1, fig. 39) is about 1.5 miles south of the Old Vanderbilt Road Bridge, but it is about 2.8 miles by the winding dirt road. Go east from Old Vanderbilt Road Bridge on the graded road continuing from Old Vanderbilt Road. About 0.1 mile east of the bridge the graded road turns sharply left (north), and a private road turns off to the right (south). Follow the graded road, first to the north, then east and south about 1.2 miles (1.3 miles past the bridge) to a fork in the road. Take the right fork here and go generally south on a rough dirt road about 1.5 miles to a grass-grown trail leading off to the right (west). There is a sign "Goslow" on a broken post at this intersection. Follow the west-trending trail about 0.3 mile to the river. Downed timber may block the trail, but you can park and walk in. Recent logging roads may cause some confusion before you get to the Goslow turnoff, but if you stick to the main-traveled road heading generally south you should come out all right.

Pigeon River Campground (site 4, fig. 42) is about 2.5 miles northeast (downstream) from Pigeon Bridge Campground (site 3, fig. 41). To get to site 4, go east from Pigeon Bridge Campground on Sturgeon Valley Road 1.3 miles to a four-corner intersection. Turn left (north) at this intersection on Round Lake Road and go north, northeast and east about 1.9 miles to the intersection with Hardwood Lake Road continuing on to the east and Twin Lake Road turning off to the left (north). Turn left on Twin Lake Road and go about 0.2 mile to the campground on the left (west) side of the road. About a mile north of the four-corner intersection you will see the Lovejoy Monument, dedicated to P. S. Lovejoy, noted Michigan conservationist.

The site at County Line Road (site 5, fig. 43) should be attempted only by anglers in excellent physical condition. Continue on Twin Lake Road past the Pigeon River Campground north, east, and northeast about 2 miles to the intersection with County Line Road. This is a rough single-track road trending east-west on the north line of Otsego County. Turn left (west) on this road and go 0.5 mile to the intersection with a road coming in from the right (north). Unless you have a four-wheel drive or a pickup with high clearance you had better park off-road at this point and walk in the rest of the way. There are some deep potholes and downed timber between here and the river. Continue westward on foot a long country mile to the end of the trail road on high ground about 200 yards from the river. There is no path down to the river, but you can climb down the steep hill and cross the low ground to the stream. Be sure to leave some kind of marker to guide you back to the road.

North of County Line Road you are in Cheboygan County, and Twin Lakes Road becomes Osmun Road. To get to Tin Bridge Public Access Site (site 6, fig. 44), go north on Osmun Road about 2.2 miles beyond the County Line Road to Cornwall Road. Turn left (west) on Cornwall Road and go about 1.7 miles to Tin Bridge.

Pine Grove Campground (site 7, fig. 45) is about 1.6 miles northwest of Tin Bridge. Starting at the intersection of Cornwall Road and Osmun Road, go north on Osmun Road about 3.5 miles to the intersection with Webb Road. Turn left (west) on Webb Road and go 0.5 mile to the intersection with a dirt road leading off to the left (south). There is a sign marking the way to the campground at this turnoff. Turn left on this dirt road and go south 0.6 mile to a fork in the road. Take the right fork and continue on this road about 2 miles to the campground.

Red Bridge (site 8, fig. 46) is about 2 miles northwest of Pine Grove Campground. Starting again at the intersection of Cornwall Road and Osmun Road, go north on Osmun Road about 3.5 miles to the intersection with Webb Road. Turn left (west) on Webb Road and go about 2 miles to Red Bridge.

Sites 6, 7, and 8 can also be reached by going east out of Wolverine on Wolverine Road. Continue east on Wolverine Road, which becomes Webb Road before it reaches Red Bridge, about 7 miles east of the town of Wolverine.

To get to Pine Grove Campground (site 7, fig. 45), continue east on Webb Road about 1.5 miles past Red Bridge to a dirt road leading off to the right (south). Follow this dirt road south 0.6 miles to a fork in the road. Take the right fork and continue on this road about 2 miles to the campground.

Starting again at Red Bridge, to get to Tin Bridge (site 6, fig. 44), go east on Webb Road about 2 miles to the intersection with Osmun Road. Turn right (south) on Osmun Road and go 3.5 miles on Osmun Road to the intersection with Cornwall Road. Turn right again (west) on Cornwall Road and go about 1.7 miles to Tin Bridge.

Site No. 1. County Parking Lot

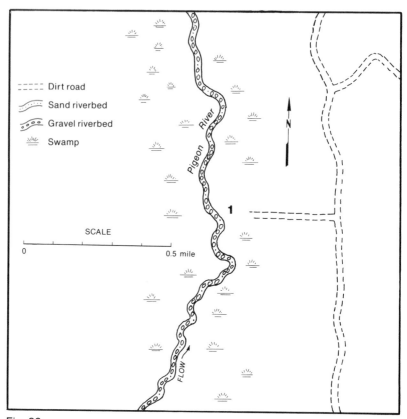

Dirt road
Sand riverbed
Gravel riverbed
Swamp

Pigeon River

N

SCALE

0   0.5 mile

1

FLOW

Fig. 39

If you want solitude, the Pigeon at the County Parking Lot is a good place for your trout fishing. Even if one or two fishermen have arrived before you, wading upstream or down 1 mile or so will usually put you alone on the river.

This part of the river is especially attractive to fishermen who prize the brook trout above all others. There are many brookies in this water, mostly small, but some over 12 inches. If you want to maintain the good fishing here you will return most or all of your catch to the water.

The Pigeon here is only 20 to 30 feet wide and seems to be even narrower because of the brushy banks. This part of the river is easier to fish with bait than with flies. The river channel is mostly less than 3 feet deep at normal flows and the bottom is mostly firm gravel, so wading is fairly easy. Stream velocity is only moderate. Trout cover is provided by the brushy overhang and by logs and snags in the channel.

Most of the river frontage is private, so stick to the channel when fishing either upstream or down from the parking lot.

Site No. 2. Old Vanderbilt Road Bridge

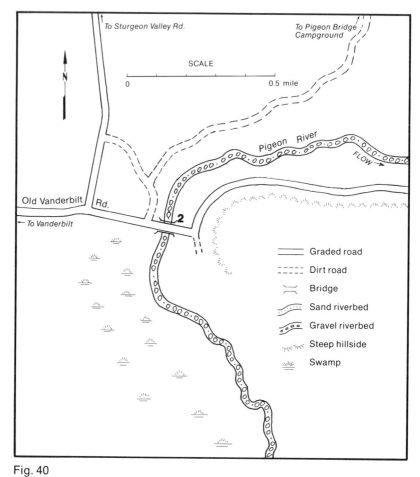

Fig. 40

The Pigeon is a little wider here than at site 1, about 35 feet, but the banks are brushy and fly casting is not easy. The riverbed is mostly gravel, channel depth is generally less than 3 feet, and wading fairly easy at normal flows. Banks are generally low and forested with mixed hardwoods and conifers.

Fishing pressure is usually light. Trout population studies here have indicated about 30 pounds of trout per acre, mostly brook trout. Except for the undeveloped public access northeast of the bridge the river frontage is all private land.

Site No. 3. Pigeon Bridge State Forest Campground

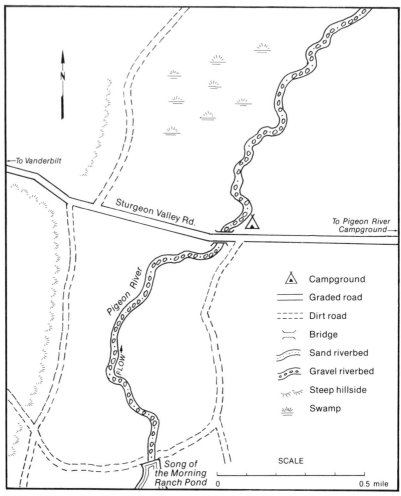

To Vanderbilt

Sturgeon Valley Rd.

To Pigeon River Campground→

Pigeon River

FLOW

Song of the Morning Ranch Pond

	Campground
	Graded road
	Dirt road
	Bridge
	Sand riverbed
	Gravel riverbed
	Steep hillside
	Swamp

SCALE

0   0.5 mile

Fig. 41

This is an attractive campground with space for seven camping parties. The campground may be crowded on weekends, but spaces usually are available the rest of the week. Although many trout fishermen camp here, fishing pressure usually is only moderate. Many of the campers come here to enjoy an informal sociability that they can no longer find in their home neighborhoods. Some of them return here each year and coordinate their vacations with those of their friends. They are friendly people and will welcome you to their ranks.

The Pigeon is a beautiful river here, flowing crystal clear between banks forested with mixed hardwoods and conifers. The channel is about 40 feet wide and generally less than 4 feet deep, with a few deeper holes. You will have to go to the banks to get by some of the deeper holes. Bottom is chiefly gravel, with some sand and muck. Velocity is moderate at normal flows. Wading is generally easy, except during periods of high runoff, which usually occur before the opening of the regular trout season. However, heavy rains can bring high water at any season.

The river is open enough for all kinds of fishing, but the fly-fisherman has it easier here than in upstream reaches. If you fish upstream from the bridge, stay in the river channel. The riverbanks upstream are private land. Downstream from the bridge, all is state land. You can fish downstream as far as you like, but carry a map and compass. If you go as much as 50 feet from the river you can find yourself hopelessly lost. Tramping a mile or more through dense timber in heavy waders can be very tiring.

Good populations of both brook and brown trout are in this part of the Pigeon, but the larger trout are more likely to be browns. DNR fish survey crews have electrofished browns up to 28 inches long in this area. More rainbow trout are also found in recent years. Good hatches of large mayflies are usually on the river in late June. One of the largest browns I have ever caught took my fly just above the bridge one warm June evening some years ago.

Site No. 4. Pigeon River State Forest Campground

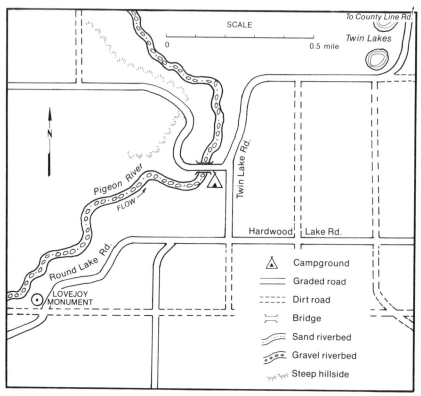

SCALE

0   0.5 mile

To County Line Rd.

Twin Lakes

Pigeon River

FLOW

Twin Lake Rd.

Hardwood Lake Rd.

Round Lake Rd.

LOVEJOY MONUMENT

N

△ Campground
═══ Graded road
----- Dirt road
⟩⟨ Bridge
∼∼ Sand riverbed
∘∘∘ Gravel riverbed
⸖⸖ Steep hillside

Fig. 42

This campground is larger than the Pigeon Bridge Campground, with space for twenty-two camping parties. Facilities are the same as at the Pigeon Bridge camp, and fishing conditions also are similar. Bottom is mostly gravel, and wading is easy, except at high flows. Watch out for in-stream logs and snags. Trout populations are about the same as at Pigeon Bridge. This is all state land—upstream and down.

Site No. 5. County Line Road

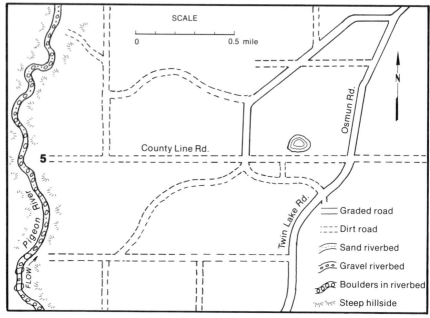

SCALE

0   0.5 mile

County Line Rd.

5

Osmun Rd.

Twin Lake Rd.

Pigeon River

FLOW

Graded road
Dirt road
Sand riverbed
Gravel riverbed
Boulders in riverbed
Steep hillside

Fig. 43

This is a remote and lonely spot, rarely visited by fishermen. Be sure to mark your trail when you climb down the steep hill to the river. The river here is a bit deeper and the flow is somewhat faster than at the upstream sites, and wading is not so easy. At high flows the river is unwadable. Upstream, the river at mid-channel is generally more than 3 feet deep, and it may overtop your waders in places. Downstream, it is generally shallower, but there are some deep holes. The Pigeon is only 35 feet wide here, but it is open enough for all kinds of fishing. Logs and snags in the river provide good trout cover, but can be a hazard to the wading fisherman, especially at night. The riverbanks are forested with mixed hardwood and conifer. Fishing pressure is light. This is all state land.

Site No. 6. Tin Bridge Public Access Site

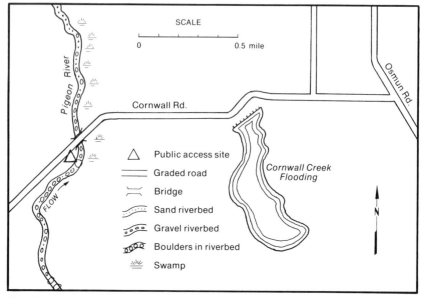

SCALE

0   0.5 mile

Pigeon River

Osmun Rd.

Cornwall Rd.

Cornwall Creek Flooding

FLOW

△   Public access site

Graded road

Bridge

Sand riverbed

Gravel riverbed

Boulders in riverbed

Swamp

N

Fig. 44

A state forest campground was formerly maintained on the west bank, upstream from the bridge. You can park on the north side of the road east of the bridge, but better off-road parking is at the old campground. The site is no longer maintained as a campground, but it is still a good access site for the fisherman. The river is 35 to 45 feet wide here and generally less than 4 feet deep, except at high flows. A few holes are more than 4 feet deep even at normal flows. Bottom is mostly gravel with some boulders. Wade with caution, watching out for large boulders, drowned logs, and snags. About a half-mile below the bridge the river gets deeper and the bottom is mostly sand. You can overtop your waders here.

There are some large fat brown trout in this water, some migrating from Mullett Lake in late summer. In mid and late season you may have this part of the river to yourself on many days. This, also, is all state land.

Site No. 7. Pine Grove State Forest Campground

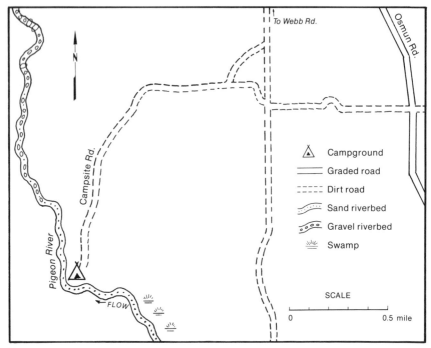

Fig. 45

This is a scenic campsite on high ground with large pine trees. The camp has a water supply, toilets, and picnic tables. Although the camp has space for only eight camping parties, it is rarely filled, except on weekends in the early season. The Pigeon is about 50 feet wide here. Going upstream from the campground the river is generally more than 4 feet deep at mid-channel and will overtop your waders in places. Downstream, it is mostly less than 4 feet deep at normal flows for about a half-mile, then becomes deeper again. The river bottom is mostly sand. The banks are generally low and brushy, but there is a steep clay bank where the path from the camp goes down to the river and large boulders are in the river at the foot of the path. You can take a fall here when the clay is wet.

Large brooks, browns, and rainbows are in this water. Brook trout up to 15 inches have been captured. This part of the river is not heavily fished, probably because wading is never easy. At high flows, wading is impossible. This is all state land upstream and nearly 1 mile downstream.

Site No. 8. Red Bridge

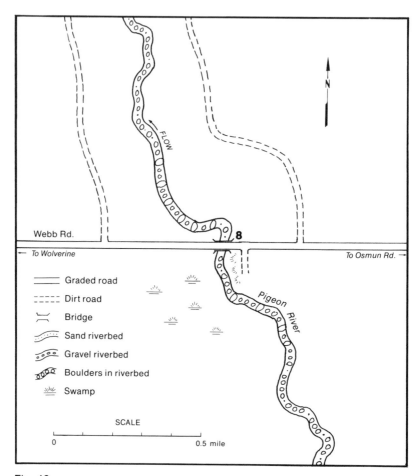

Fig. 46

Park on the north side of the road west of the bridge. The river is about 50 feet wide here and less than 4 feet deep in most places at low flows. The bottom is gravel and boulders. The banks are alternately high and low, forested with hardwoods. The river is wide enough and open enough for easy fly casting, but wading can be difficult because of the swift flow and slippery cobbles and boulders. At high flows, wading is dangerous to impossible. There is some state land at the bridge, but most land, upstream and down, is private.

Sturgeon River

The Sturgeon River north of Gaylord is one of the best streams for large lake-run brown trout in Michigan. It also has brook trout in the upper reaches and lake-run rainbows in the lower river. Most of the larger trout are caught in the lower river, where a swift flow and deep holes make wading difficult, and, in places, impossible. The upper river is easier to wade, but the fish run smaller. However, some large lake-run browns enter the upper river in late summer. The narrow channel, deep holes, and fast current in the lower river favor the bank fisherman, and bait and spin fishermen generally have an advantage over the fly-fisherman here.

The headwaters of the Sturgeon, like those of the Pigeon and Black to the east, front the northern slope of the moraine left by the Port Huron ice sheet some 13,000 years ago. The crest of this moraine forms the divide between these north-flowing streams and the Au Sable drainage on the south. From the headwaters the Sturgeon flows northward 36 river miles to discharge into Burt Lake at Indian River.

From the headwaters to Sturgeon Bridge, about 10 river miles, the Sturgeon is a small stream, generally less than 30 feet wide and 3 feet deep, with mostly sand bottom. Most of it is shallow enough to wade, but logjams, snags, and drowned logs are hazards to the wading fisherman. The narrow channel and brushy banks make fly-fishing difficult. On the positive side, you have a good chance to fish alone on this part of the river.

Probably the best part of the river for the fly-fisherman is the 10 river miles that extends from Sturgeon Bridge downstream to Trowbridge Road. The upper part of this water formerly was private property, off limits to most fishermen, but is now owned by the state and open to public fishing. The river bottom is mostly sand at Sturgeon Bridge but gravel becomes more abundant downstream, and at Trowbridge Road the bottom is almost entirely gravel and boulders. The width of the river varies from 30 to 50 feet and the depth is mostly less than 4 feet at normal flows, with some deeper runs. Drowned logs and snags downstream from Sturgeon Bridge provide good cover but make wading difficult. The river is more open and cover somewhat sparse as you approach Trowbridge Road.

From Trowbridge Road downstream to Haakwood Campground, about 6 river miles, the bottom is mostly gravel and boulders, the flow is swift, and wading is difficult at all times. Some of this water cannot be waded even at low flows. At high flows, almost all of it is unwadable. The West Branch of the Sturgeon comes in at Wolverine, greatly increasing the flow. Most of the river above Wolverine is less than 4 feet deep at normal flows, but there are some deeper runs. Below Wolverine some of the holes are over your head. The river varies in width from about 30 to 60 feet. The narrow reaches are the most difficult and the most dangerous for the wading fisherman.

The Sturgeon River near Sturgeon Bridge

From Haakwood Campground to the mouth at Burt Lake, about 10 river miles, the Sturgeon is mostly too fast and too deep for safe wading. The river is 35 to 70 feet wide and mostly 3 to 6 feet deep. Bottom is mostly gravel, with some hard, slippery clay below the campground and some sand near the mouth. Edge wading is possible in places, but most fishing is done from the banks.

Unlike the Pigeon, very little of the Sturgeon flows through public lands, but access to the river is provided at numerous bridges and public access sites. A fisherman can find solitude and a near-wilderness atmosphere in some of the upstream reaches. Below Trowbridge Road, the river flows close to major highways, and it is difficult to escape the sights and sounds of civilization. If you are content to catch trout of moderate size in a small, clear stream, so long as you can have the water all to yourself, you may find what you want in the upper river. If you want the larger trout that run upriver from Burt Lake, try the lower Sturgeon.

Boat fishing on the Sturgeon, except for the quiet water near the mouth, is not feasible. The flow is too fast to allow the fisherman to adequately cover the water, whether with bait, spinner, or fly. Neither is the Sturgeon well suited for recreational canoeing. The upper river is hard going because of the narrow channel and many logjams, and the lower river is not safe for inexperienced boaters. Nevertheless, a moderate canoe traffic has developed on the lower river in recent years. Spills are not uncommon, and the results could be tragic.

The Sturgeon is a cold stream, colder than the Pigeon or Black, and has a relatively large flow during dry periods. Gravel beds are sparse in the upper river but are abundant in most of the stream below the Green Timbers property. The river would appear to offer almost ideal trout habitat, but trout populations and spawning success are relatively low, probably because of the high levels of sand bed load in the stream. Work is now underway to improve trout habitat on the Sturgeon, first by stabilizing stream banks and other erodable areas in the watershed and second by constructing sedimentation basins where the sand can be trapped and removed (Swan 1984).

Fluctuations in stage most years are less than 2 feet, but the generally high velocity of flow can make even a small rise dangerous to the wading fisherman. Midstream velocities at low flow in several parts of the river ranged from 1 to 4.5 feet per second. A velocity of

3 feet per second makes dangerous wading where the water is more than 3 feet deep.

Accommodations

The fisherman can find ample accommodations at many cabins and motels in Gaylord, Vanderbilt, Wolverine, and Indian River. Fishing equipment is also available in each of these towns, and numerous grocery stores supply the campers.

Burt Lake State Park near the mouth of the Sturgeon has all modern facilities for 137 camping parties. More primitive but adequate accommodations for 18 camping parties are provided at the Haakwood State Forest Campground on the Sturgeon 2 miles north (downstream) from Winchester.

Maps of the Sturgeon

The access sites on the Sturgeon are easier to find than those on the Pigeon or Black. Most of the secondary roads run along section lines, and there are few unmarked trail roads. The location maps (figs. 47 and 48) show the stream channel and public roads leading to the river.

Ten access sites are numbered on these maps in downstream order.

The first site at Poquette Road Bridge (fig. 49) can be reached by driving north from Gaylord on Old U.S. 27. Go north exactly 3 miles from the center of the town to the intersection with Poquette Road. Turn right (east) on the blacktop Poquette Road and go about 1.7 miles to the bridge.

The next access site downstream is Doc Sehls Bridge (fig. 50). Go back (west) on Poquette Road to Old U.S. 27. Turn right (north) on 27 and go about 3.5 miles to the intersection with Whitmarsh Road. Turn right (east) on Whitmarsh and go about 3.4 miles to the bridge. Or, starting from Vanderbilt, go south on Old U.S. 27 about 1.9 miles to the intersection with Whitmarsh Road. Turn left (east) on Whitmarsh and go about 3.4 miles to the bridge.

Old Vanderbilt Road Bridge (site 3, fig. 51) is about 1.5 miles downstream from Doc Sehls Bridge. Go east out of Vanderbilt on Sturgeon Valley Road about 3.5 miles to the intersection with Old

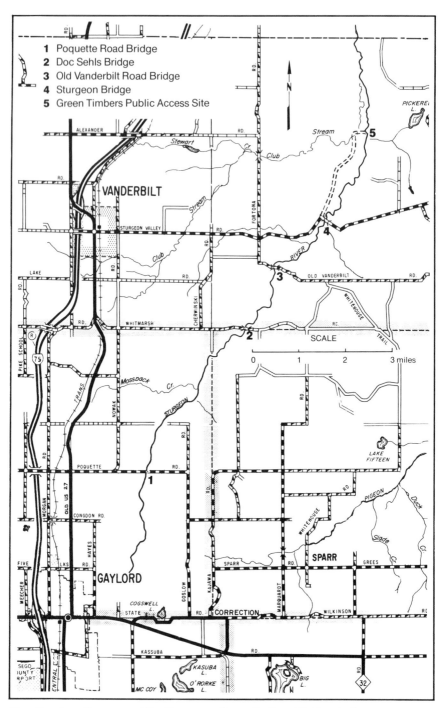

1 Poquette Road Bridge
2 Doc Sehls Bridge
3 Old Vanderbilt Road Bridge
4 Sturgeon Bridge
5 Green Timbers Public Access Site

Fig. 47.   Location map of the Sturgeon, Poquette Road Bridge to Green Timbers Public Access Site

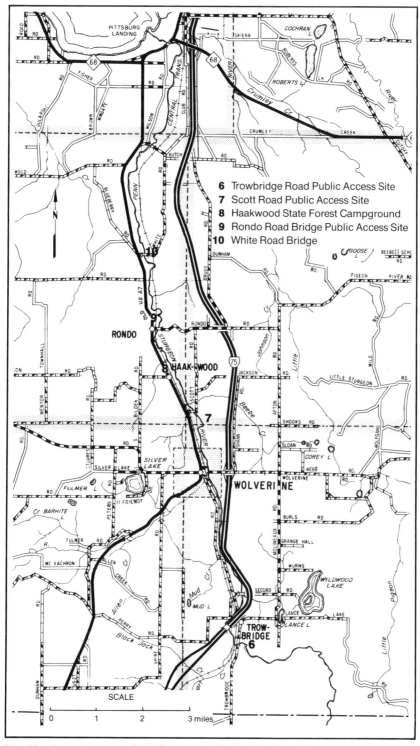

6 Trowbridge Road Public Access Site
7 Scott Road Public Access Site
8 Haakwood State Forest Campground
9 Rondo Road Bridge Public Access Site
10 White Road Bridge

Fig. 48. Location map of the Sturgeon, Trowbridge Road Public Access Site to White Road Bridge

Vanderbilt Road. Turn right (south) on Old Vanderbilt Road and go south and east about 1 mile to the bridge.

Sturgeon Bridge (site 4, fig. 52) is on the blacktop Sturgeon Valley Road about 5.3 miles east of Vanderbilt.

The Green Timbers area (site 5, fig. 53) is just downstream (north) from Sturgeon Bridge. You cannot drive into Green Timbers, but you can park your car near the gate about 0.1 mile west of Sturgeon Bridge and walk down to the river.

Site 6 (fig. 54) is a public access site near the south bridge on Trowbridge Road. Go south out of Wolverine on Trowbridge Road about 3.5 miles to a dirt road turning off to the left (east). You will cross the first bridge over the Sturgeon about 3 miles south of Wolverine and will pass under I-75 before you get to the turnoff, which is about 0.1 mile north of the second bridge. Turn left on the rough dirt road and go east and south about 0.3 mile to the public access on the river.

Scott Road Public Access Site (site 7, fig. 55) is near the first

The Sturgeon River near Green Timbers

bridge on the Sturgeon downstream from Wolverine. Go north out of Wolverine on Old U.S. 27 about 1.3 miles and turn right on Scott Road. Go east on this road about 0.2 mile to the bridge. Cross the bridge and turn right (south) on a dirt road and follow this road another 0.2 mile to the access site on the right (east) bank of the river.

Haakwood Campground (site 8, fig. 56) is on the left (west) bank of the Sturgeon about 0.8 mile downstream from Scott Bridge. Go north out of Wolverine on Old U.S. 27 about 2.1 miles and turn right (east) on the campground road across the railroad tracks to the campground. Stop and look before you cross the tracks.

Site 9 (fig. 57) is a public access site north of Rondo Road Bridge. Go north out of Wolverine on Old U.S. 27 about 3.2 miles to Rondo Road. Continue north another 0.3 mile to a dirt road leading off to the right (east). Turn right on this winding road and follow it down 0.4 mile to the access site on the river.

White Road Bridge (site 10, fig. 58) is about 1.5 miles north of Rondo Bridge. Go north out of Wolverine on Old U.S. 27 about 4.7 miles to the intersection with White Road. Turn right (east) on White Road and go about 0.1 mile to the bridge.

Site No. 1. Poquette Road Bridge

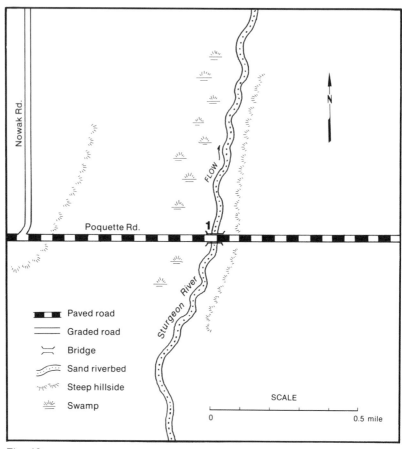

Fig. 49

The Sturgeon is a small brook here, 20 to 30 feet wide and mostly less than 3 feet deep. Bottom is mostly sand. Wading is fairly easy at normal flows, but fly casting is difficult because of the narrow channel and overhanging branches. The banks are low and mucky, lined mostly with conifers, some brush, and a few grassy areas near streamside cabins. Studies by the DNR have indicated a high trout population here, but they are mostly small fish. Brooks, browns, and small rainbows are caught here. Except for the road right-of-way, this is all private land. This part of the river is easier fished with bait than with either flies or spinning lures.

Site No. 2. Doc Sehls Bridge

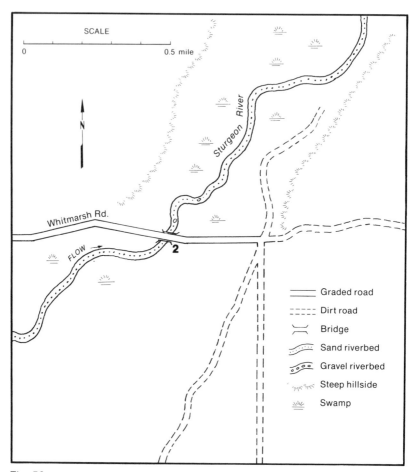

Fig. 50

The Sturgeon is still a small stream here, 20 to 30 feet wide and mostly 2 to 3 feet deep. Bottom is predominately sand with a few small patches of gravel and some muck along the banks. The low banks are lined with swamp conifer, some brush and grassy areas. Wading and fishing conditions are similar to those at Poquette Road Bridge. Fishing pressure usually is light. All river frontage is private, except for the road right-of-way.

Site No. 3. Old Vanderbilt Road Bridge

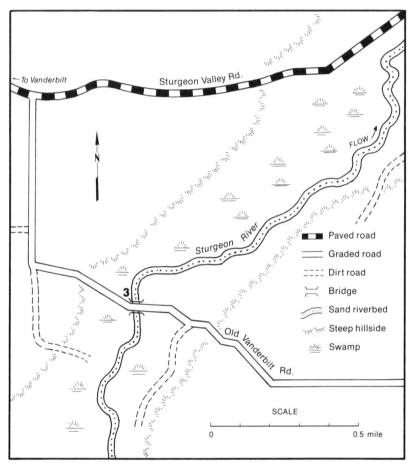

Fig. 51

There is room to park one or two cars on the north side of the road west of the bridge. The Sturgeon is a bit wider here, 30 to 35 feet wide, and mostly 2 to 3 feet deep, with some deeper holes. Velocity is moderate. Bottom is mostly sand. Wading is easy at normal flows, but the brushy banks make flycasting difficult. The banks are low and brushy, lined with swamp conifers. State land extends upstream about one-fourth mile on both sides of the river. Downstream, there is state land on the right (east) bank, but the left bank is private. This segment usually is not heavily fished.

Site No. 4. Sturgeon Bridge

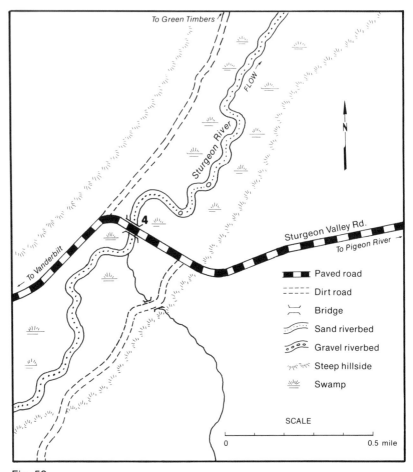

Fig. 52

The Sturgeon is 35 to 45 feet wide here and 2 to 3 feet deep, with some deeper holes. The bottom is mostly sand with some muck. The banks are low, forested with mixed hardwood and conifer. Wading is fairly easy at normal flows, but watch out for drowned logs, snags, and holes. Velocity of flow is moderate. The river is open enough in places to cast a fly. The trout here average substantially larger than in the upstream reaches. Trout cover along fallen logs and snags is adequate. There is room to park two or three cars on both sides of the road east of the bridge. Downstream from the bridge is the Green Timbers property, now owned by the state. Upstream, all property is private.

Site No. 5. Green Timbers Public Access Site

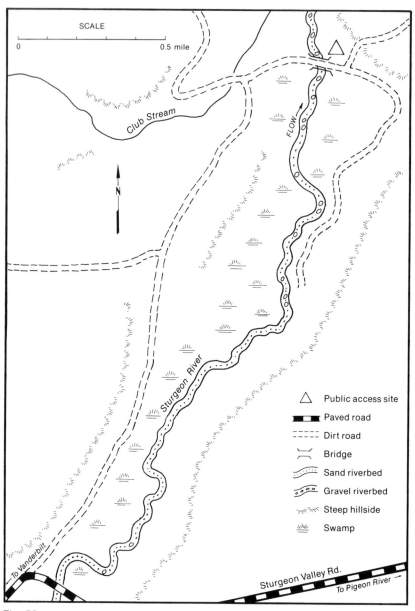

SCALE

0   0.5 mile

Club Stream

FLOW

N

Sturgeon River

To Vanderbilt

Sturgeon Valley Rd.

To Pigeon River

△ Public access site

▓▓ Paved road

- - - - Dirt road

≍ Bridge

Sand riverbed

○○○ Gravel riverbed

Steep hillside

Swamp

Fig. 53

158 • **Sturgeon River**

Before 1982, Green Timbers was private property and off limits to most fishermen. Now owned by the state, Green Timbers offers some of the best fishing for resident trout on the Sturgeon. Motorized vehicles are not permitted on the Green Timbers property, but walk-in access is allowed to any part of the property, beginning at Sturgeon Valley Road and extending several miles downstream. There is room to park your car on the north side of Sturgeon Valley Road just west of the gate to the service road. The service road parallels the river on the west about 2.3 miles to the wood bridge near the lodge. You can walk down this road and cross over to fish any part of the river. The farther you walk, the better your chances of fishing alone.

The Sturgeon here is 30 to 50 feet wide and 2 to 4 feet deep, with some deeper holes. The river bottom is almost all soft sand and muck near Sturgeon Valley Road, but patches of gravel appear as you approach the lodge, and gravel predominates as you near the north line of Otsego County. Logs and snags in the water provide good trout cover. The banks are generally low and mucky upstream but become higher and sandy near the lower end. Tree cover is mostly swamp conifer in the upper part, hardwood upland in the lower. There are some brushy areas and some open grassland.

Wading is fairly easy if you watch out for snags and logs in the water. Overhanging branches are a problem in some of the narrower parts, but most of this area is open enough for fly casting. Velocity of flow is only moderate at normal flows, so upstream wading is not too difficult. Fishing pressure is very light. Good numbers of lake-run browns enter this area in early fall. Some fish travel all the way up to the Poquette Road site to spawn.

Site No. 6. Trowbridge Road Public Access Site

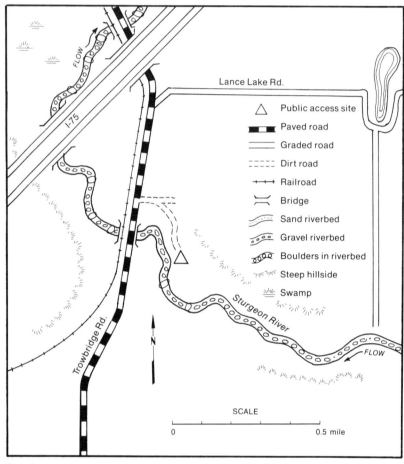

Fig. 54

The fishing here is quite different from that in the upstream access sites. The flow is swift and the slippery cobbles and boulders make wading more difficult. The river is narrow, 30 to 40 feet wide, and mostly 2 to 4 feet deep, with some deeper runs. There is a low-head rock dam about halfway between the access site and the bridge. If you wade downstream about a half-mile you will come to rapids and deeper water that you probably should avoid. At high flows, none of this water is wadable. The banks are low and brushy, with open grassland and some hardwoods. Trout cover is good. Although narrow, the river is open enough for fly casting. Fishing pressure is usually light to moderate. The access site has space for parking several cars and one outdoor toilet but no other facilities.

Site No. 7. Scott Road Public Access Site

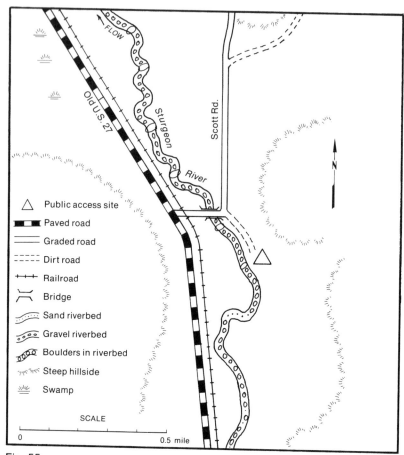

Public access site

Paved road

Graded road

Dirt road

Railroad

Bridge

Sand riverbed

Gravel riverbed

Boulders in riverbed

Steep hillside

Swamp

SCALE

0   0.5 mile

Fig. 55

Camping is no longer permited at this public access site. There is one outdoor toilet and room to park several cars, but no other facilities. The river is 40 to 55 feet wide and mostly 2 to 4 feet deep at normal flows, with some deeper runs. If you wade upstream from the access site you will come to some deeper water that may overtop your waders. The flow is swift and there are slippery rocks and boulders here, but you can wade some of this water with care at normal low flows. Felt-soled boots probably would be helpful. The banks are low, sandy, and brushy, with some larger hardwoods and open grassland. The river is open enough for easy fly casting. Trout cover is somewhat sparse. Fishing pressure usually is moderate. During spawning runs it may be heavy.

Site No. 8. Haakwood State Forest Campground

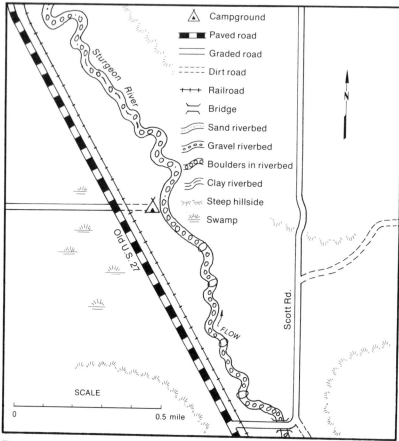

Fig. 56

Now a state forest campground, this was formerly a public access site where camping was permitted. Called "the old orchard" by some of the early users, the site was popular with fishermen during the spring and fall spawning runs and with other vacationers during holiday weekends. The campground still is used by fishermen, but probably not so much as in the old days. There are designated spaces for eighteen camping parties in two areas, one north and one south of the entrance road.

The river is 50 to 60 feet wide and mostly 2 to 4 feet deep, with some deeper holes at the bends. Bottom is mostly gravel, with some boulders and patches of hard, slippery clay. The banks are sandy, alternately high and low, and forested with hardwood, including some old apple trees. This is fast water, and wading is difficult to impossible. Most fishermen stick to the quieter shallows or fish from the banks. There is room for fly casting, but most fishermen here use bait or spinning lures. This area is heavily fished during the spawning runs.

Site No. 9. Rondo Road Bridge
Public Access Site

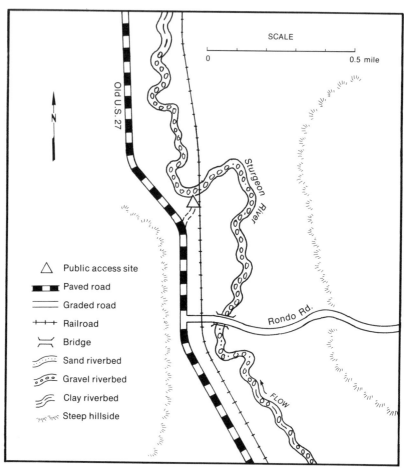

SCALE

0   0.5 mile

N

Old U.S. 27

Sturgeon River

Rondo Rd.

FLOW

△ Public access site

▬▬▬ Paved road

═══ Graded road

+++++ Railroad

⨞ Bridge

Sand riverbed

Gravel riverbed

Clay riverbed

Steep hillside

Fig. 57

There are two parking areas here, one by the bridge and one at the public access site about 0.3 mile north of the bridge. The Sturgeon is about 50 feet wide here. It is mostly less than 4 feet deep upstream from the bridge, but it is fast water, and wading is difficult to impossible. Downstream from the bridge most of the river is too deep and fast for wading. Bottom is mostly gravel with some sand. Banks are alternately high and low and are covered with hardwood trees, brush, and some open grassy areas. Most of the fishing here is done from the banks, usually with bait or spinning lures. Fishing pressure is light except during the spawning runs. The only public land here is the road right-of-way at the bridge and for about one-fourth mile at the public access site to the north.

Site No. 10. White Road Bridge

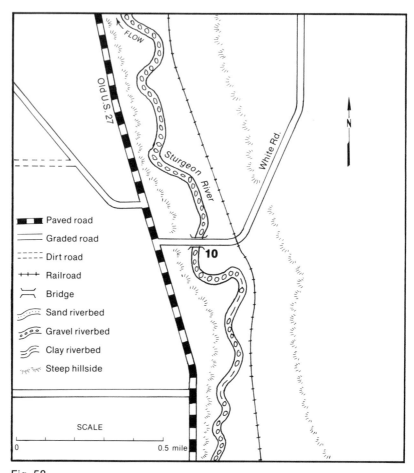

Fig. 58

The river is narrow, fast, and deep here. It is about 40 feet wide and too fast and deep for safe wading. Fishing usually is done from the banks with bait or spinning lures. The banks are high, sandy, and covered with brush and hardwood timber. The stream bottom is chiefly gravel. Fishing pressure may be heavy during the spawning runs, but is light the rest of the season. Except for the road right-of-way, this is all private land.

Black River

The Black River northeast of Gaylord is rated one of the best brook-trout streams in Michigan's Lower Peninsula. The Black is the easternmost of the three streams that rise on the north slope of the moraine near Gaylord. The Black is the most remote from I-75 and a large part of the upper river is not open to public fishing. Because of this it is not heavily fished, and some of the brook trout reach a large size. It is not a popular canoe trail, and very few people camp on the river, although camping is permitted at two of the public access sites.

The Black is a first-class trout stream from its headwaters all the way to Tower Pond, a distance of about 44 river miles. From its source to Tin Shanty Bridge, about 11 river miles, the Black is a narrow, brushy stream, generally less than 30 feet wide and shallow enough in most places for easy wading. The brush overhanging the channel makes fly casting difficult, and this part of the river is better suited to bait and spin fishing. The banks are low here, and back of the brush are cedars and other swamp conifers. Most of the river upstream from Tin Shanty Bridge flows through state land, but developed access sites are few.

Downstream from Tin Shanty Bridge the Black widens and is open enough for fly-fishing. From Tin Shanty Bridge to the east line of Otsego County, about 3 river miles, most of the riverfront is state land and open to public fishing. The river is 30 to 50 feet wide, mostly less than 4 feet deep, and the bottom is mostly gravel with some sand. Some upland hardwoods appear in this reach, and hardwoods become more abundant downstream. This is a pleasant part of the river to fish, deep enough to hold some good trout but not so deep as to make difficult wading.

From the east line of Otsego County (west line of Montmorency County) downstream to Clark Bridge, about 12 river miles, the Black flows through large private holdings, and public access is very limited. There is some state frontage at the upper end east of Town Corner Lake Campground and at the lower end near Clark Bridge. The only other public access is the road right-of-way at Main River Bridge, at the north boundary of Black River Ranch. You can float the river from Tin Shanty Bridge to Main River Bridge, but do not try to float it from Main River Bridge to Clark Bridge. The river divides into several narrow channels too small to float a canoe at the "spreads" on the Black River property, and you cannot portage without trespassing on private property.

This part of the river is 30 to 80 feet wide and mostly 2 to 4 feet deep. There are some deeper holes and one reach, about a half-mile long, of deeper water just above the spreads. The bottom is sand and gravel in the upper part and mostly sand in the lower. Banks are alternately high and low in the upper part, forested with mixed hardwood and conifer. In the lower part the banks are mostly low with hardwood forest, some brush, and open grassland.

The Black River near the South Tower Public Access Site

From Clark Bridge to Crocket Bridge, about 6 river miles, the Black flows through large areas of state land, but road access to the river is limited. The river bottom is mostly sand at Clark Bridge, but gravel becomes more abundant downstream, and gravel and boulders make up most of the river bottom at Crocket Bridge. The river is 60 to 80 feet wide and generally 1 to 4 feet deep, with some deeper parts. This section of the river can be floated at normal flows by canoeists of moderate competence. There are some rapids and shallow riffles that may bump the bottom at low flows. The river-banks are mostly low, with hardwood swamp and some brush.

From Crocket Bridge to Tower Pond, about 12 river miles, most of the Black is too deep to wade, and boat fishing is more popular here. However, parts are wadable at low flows, and edge wading is possible in some of the deeper areas. There is some state land in the upper part of this section and several easements for public fishing on private land downstream. The river here is 60 to 80 feet wide and generally 3 to 6 feet deep, with some shallower reaches. Bottom is chiefly gravel in the shallower reaches and sand and muck in the deeper parts. The banks are mostly low, forested with hardwoods.

The population of brook trout in the upper Black indicates a good trout habitat. In 1991, brook trout populations at several sites averaged about 24 pounds per acre (Fenske 1992). Populations ranged from a high of about 51 pounds per acre at McKinnon Bend to a low of about 7 pounds per acre at Tin Shanty Bridge. The discharge of the Black is relatively stable, with enough groundwater inflow to sustain the river during dry periods. There are some sandy areas, but most of the river has gravel bottom for spawning beds. The river is too warm in summer for ideal trout water, warmer than the Sturgeon, for example, but the trout seem to thrive, nevertheless. Like other streams in the area, the water in the Black is hard, slightly alkaline, with sufficient nutrients to support a good trout population, but not so much as to stimulate an undesirable growth of aquatic vegetation. Fluctuations in stage on the Black, usually about 2 feet in a normal year, are enough to make drastic changes in wading conditions. Waters that are easily waded at low flows can overtop your waders or sweep you off your feet when the river is high.

The Black was known for its grayling fishing before it became famous as a trout stream. According to William B. Mershon (1923), the grayling held out longer on the Black than on the Au

Sable. He tells of a four-day fishing trip on the Black in 1903 when a party of seven caught 46 grayling and 346 brook trout. The Black has been noted for its trout fishing, especially brook-trout fishing, ever since. The river can maintain this brook-trout fishery only if it is protected from degradation of the stream itself and from overkill of the trout. The recent oil and gas development in the upper river has already caused some deterioration of the wilderness atmosphere. Because brook trout are relatively easy to catch it may be desirable to impose special regulations on the Black to limit the kill of trout.

Accommodations

Lodging for fishermen is available at many motels in Onaway and Gaylord. There are also many excellent restaurants in these towns. Fishing tackle can be purchased from sporting goods and hardware stores in these towns and in the village of Tower.

Two state forest campgrounds are near, but not on, the river. Round Lake Campground is about 1.5 miles north of McKinnon Bend. Town Corner Lake Campground is about 2.5 miles southeast of Tin Shanty Bridge. Round Lake Campground has space for six and Town Corner Lake Campground has space for twelve camping parties. Both campgrounds are equipped with water supply and outdoor toilets. Spaces are usually available at both campgrounds, even on weekends. Camping is also permitted at two public access sites.

Maps of the Black

The location maps (figs. 59 and 60) show the river channel of the Black and roads leading to it. Some new roads associated with recent oil and gas development are not shown on the maps, and a few of the roads shown are not open to the public.

The seven access sites shown on the map are numbered in downstream order. Some of the upstream sites are not easy to find, and the new pipeline roads add to the confusion. The directions given are not always the shortest routes to the sites, but they should be the easiest to follow.

A starting point for the first three sites on the upper Black is Tin Shanty Bridge. To reach Tin Shanty Bridge, drive east from

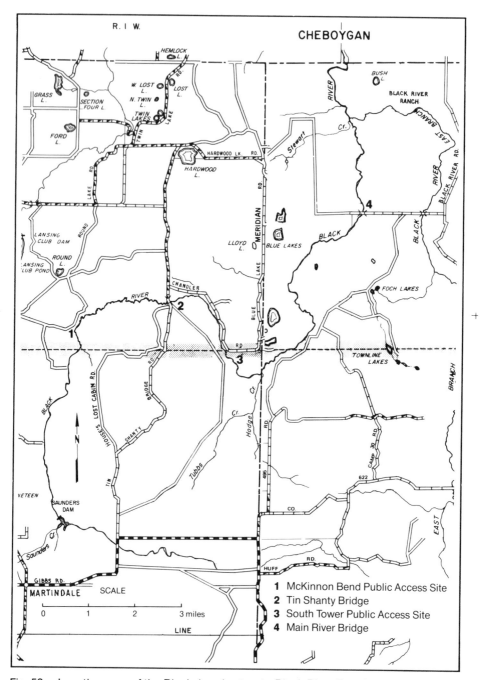

Fig. 59.   Location map of the Black, headwaters to Black River Ranch

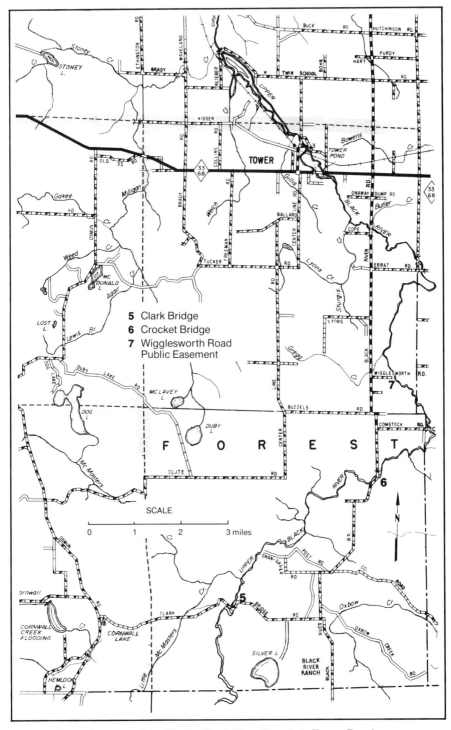

5 Clark Bridge
6 Crocket Bridge
7 Wigglesworth Road
  Public Easement

Fig. 60. Location map of the Black, Black River Ranch to Tower Road

Gaylord on M-32. About 1 mile east of Gaylord, M-32 angles off to the right (south), but you turn off to the left and continue straight east on the blacktop Wilkinson Road another 3.4 miles to the intersection with Marquardt Road. Turn left (north) on the black-top Marquardt Road and go 1 mile to the intersection with Sparr Road. Turn right on Sparr Road (also blacktop) and go east about 7.3 miles to the point where the blacktop turns left (north). Sparr Road becomes Gibbs Road before you get to this turn. Go left (north) with the blacktop about 0.7 mile to the point where the blacktop turns right (east) again. You do not turn right, but con-tinue north on the rough graded road called Tin Shanty Bridge Road. This road winds generally north 5.7 miles to Tin Shanty Bridge. The road goes through dense hardwood forest and in places is not wide enough for two cars to pass. Watch out for fast-moving logging trucks. Two dirt roads turn off from Tin Shanty Bridge Road before you get to the bridge. Sawdust Pile Road turns off to the right about 0.5 mile north of Gibbs Road, and House's Lost Cabin Road turns off to the left about 1.5 miles north of Sawdust Pile Road. However, both of these roads come back to Tin Shanty Bridge Road before it reaches the bridge.

Tin Shanty Bridge is site 2 (fig. 62) on your map. To get to McKinnon Bend Public Access Site (site 1, fig. 61), go north from Tin Shanty Bridge about 1 mile to a dirt road leading off to the left (west). Turn left on this road and follow it west and southwest about 2.5 miles to an intersection at Round Lake Campground. Turn left (southeast) at this intersection and follow the dirt road generally south 1.6 miles to a sharp bend to the right (west). The access site is just to the left of this bend.

Site 3 (fig. 63) is an undeveloped public access site about 1.5 miles southeast of Tin Shanty Bridge. Go north from Tin Shanty Bridge about 0.3 mile, then turn right (east) on a dirt road and follow this road east and then southeast about 2.2 miles. Here the road turns left (east) again, but you turn off into the parking area on your right.

You can go east from site 3 to Blue Lake Road, then north and east again to the downstream access sites, but this is not an easy route to follow. Some of the crossover roads are not open to the public. For your first visit to the area I suggest you approach these downstream sites from the village of Onaway.

Wigglesworth Road Public Easement (site 7, fig. 67) is about 5 miles southwest of Onaway. Go west out of Onaway toward Tower on M-68 about 2 miles to the intersection with Black River Road. Turn left (south) on this road and go about 4.2 miles to Wigglesworth Road turning off to the left (east). Turn left on Wigglesworth Road and drive down about 0.5 mile to the access site on the river.

Crocket Bridge (site 6, fig. 66) is about 2.1 miles south of Wigglesworth Road. Continue south on Black River Road from Wigglesworth Road 2.1 miles to the bridge.

Clark Bridge (site 5, fig. 65) is about 4 miles southwest of Crocket Bridge. Continue south and west from Crocket Bridge on Black River Road about 3.6 miles to a T intersection with Clark Bridge Road. Turn right (west) on Clark Bridge Road and go about 2.1 miles to Clark Bridge.

Main River Bridge (site 4, fig. 64) is about 5 miles south of Clark Bridge. Go back past the T intersection of Clark Bridge Road with Black River Road and turn right (south) on Black River Road. Continue south on Black River Road about 4.9 miles to an intersection with a dirt road leading off to the right (west). Turn right on this road and go about 1.8 mile to Main River Bridge. You will cross the East Branch of the Black River on Barber Bridge before you get to Main River Bridge on the mainstream.

Site No. 1. McKinnon Bend Public Access Site

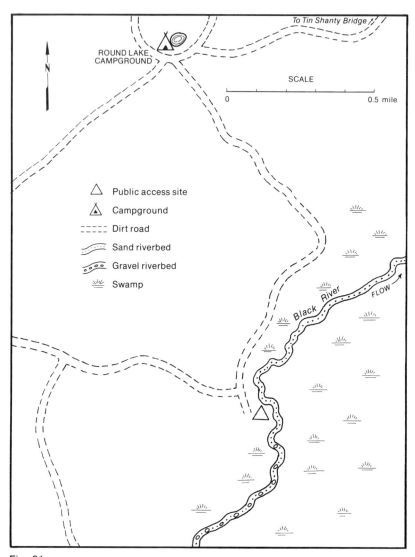

To Tin Shanty Bridge

ROUND LAKE CAMPGROUND

SCALE

0   0.5 mile

N

△ Public access site

▲ Campground

- - - - Dirt road

　　Sand riverbed

○○○ Gravel riverbed

Swamp

Black River

FLOW

Fig. 61

The Black is about 20 feet wide here, but the heavy brush on the banks makes it appear even narrower. The channel is generally less than 4 feet deep, with a few deeper holes. The bottom is mostly sand with a few small patches of gravel. It is frustrating to try to cast a fly in this water, but some fishermen manage it. Bait and spin fishermen have an easier time of it. Wading is fairly easy at normal flows. There is state land on both banks at the public access site, but some private land upstream and down. The banks are low and swampy, covered with brush, some open grassland, and scattered trees. It is easy to get lost here, so carry a compass and map. This is good brook-trout water, usually not heavily fished. If you want solitude you can usually find it here. Although camping is permitted, few camp here during the trout season. In 1991 there were more brook trout over 8 inches in this water than recorded at any other site on the Black.

Site No. 2. Tin Shanty Bridge

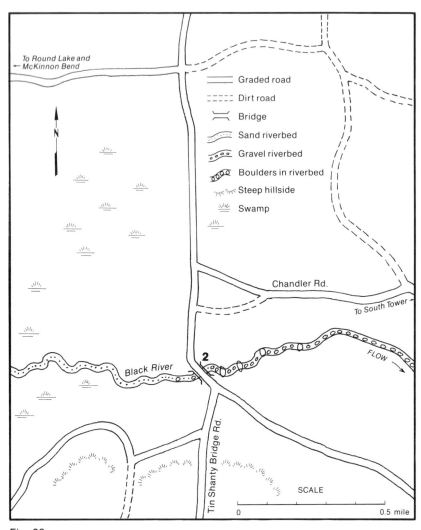

Fig. 62

There is very little room to park on the narrow shoulder at the bridge. A better parking area is at an abandoned gravel pit on the east side of the road about 200 yards south of the bridge. The river is 30 to 40 feet wide and generally less than 4 feet deep, with some deeper holes. The bottom is mostly gravel and boulders at the bridge and downstream. Upstream, it is chiefly sand. The banks are a little higher than in the upstream reaches, not so swampy, and not so brushy. Fly casting is easier here. Wading is fairly easy, also, at normal flows, but watch out for the holes, boulders, and snags. State lands are on both sides of the river at the bridge and upstream. Downstream, part of the land is state and part private. There is a low dam at the Beaver Dam Club about 0.7 mile downstream from the bridge. This is good brook-trout water, with plenty of state land for access without trespassing on private property. Fishing pressure usually is light to moderate.

Site No. 3. South Tower Public Access Site

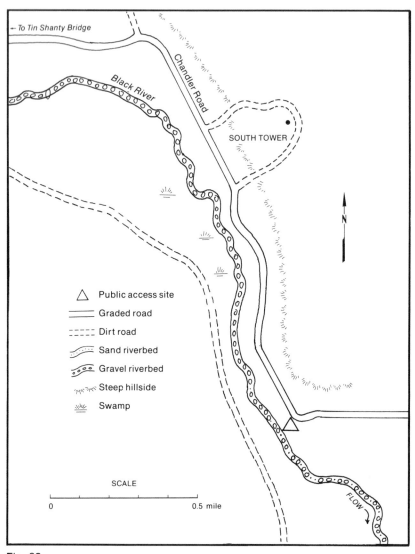

Fig. 63

Camping is permitted at this undeveloped public access site, but it is rarely used. There is a large parking area here in a pleasant grove of jack pine, maple, popple, and spruce. The high, sandy banks are vulnerable to erosion, so be careful to tread lightly when entering or leaving the river.

The river is 35 to 45 feet wide at this access site and not so brushy as it is upstream. It is mostly less than 4 feet deep, with a few deeper holes. Some of these are over your wader tops. Velocity is moderate, and wading is easy at normal flows. Drowned logs and snags make good trout cover. The bottom is mostly gravel upstream, sand and gravel downstream. The left bank (northeast side) is high and sandy, the right bank low and mucky. This is one of the best places on the river for the fly-fisherman, but it usually is not heavily fished. State land on both banks extends a quarter-mile upstream and down.

Site No. 4. Main River Bridge

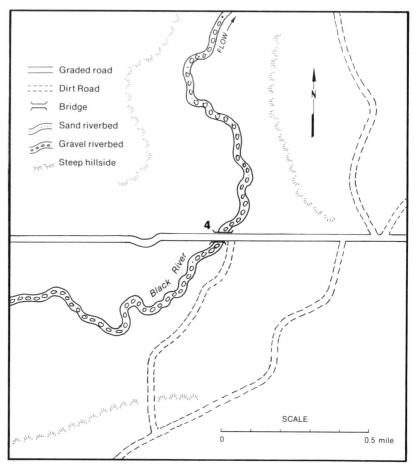

Graded road
Dirt Road
Bridge
Sand riverbed
Gravel riverbed
Steep hillside

FLOW

N

4

Black River

SCALE

0

0.5 mile

Fig. 64

The road right-of-way at this bridge is the only public access to the river for several miles, upstream and down. The private club called Black River Ranch is downstream from the bridge, and Blue Lakes Club and other private holdings are upstream. There is very limited parking on the narrow shoulders near the bridge. Do not block the entrance to the Gaylord Fishing Club on the south side of the road. The river is about 35 feet wide here and mostly 2 to 4 feet deep, with some deeper holes. Bottom is mostly gravel, with some sand and muck. Velocity is moderate to fast. Upstream from the bridge the banks are high and sandy, with hardwood forest. Downstream, the banks are low and brushy, with some open grassland. The river is open enough for fly casting and wading is fairly easy, except at high flows. Fishing pressure usually is light.

Site No. 5. Clark Bridge

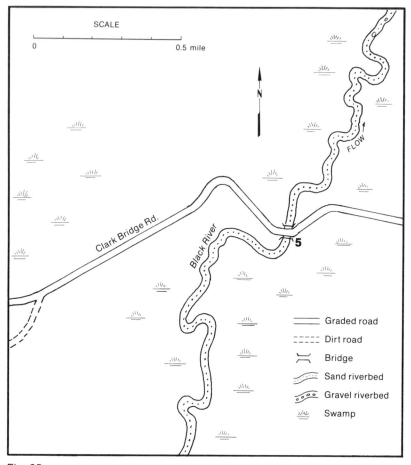

SCALE

0   0.5 mile

N

FLOW

Clark Bridge Rd.

Black River

5

Graded road

Dirt road

Bridge

Sand riverbed

Gravel riverbed

Swamp

Fig. 65

There is ample off-road parking north of the road east of the bridge. Upstream from the bridge, the river is 70 to 80 feet wide and generally 2 to 4 feet deep, with some deeper holes. Downstream, it is mostly too deep to wade. A deep hole just below the bridge will overtop your waders. Velocity is moderate to fast. The bottom is mostly sand. The banks are low and mucky, forested with hardwood and some brush. The river above the bridge can be waded at normal flows. At high flows wading may be difficult to impossible. There is plenty of room to fish with bait, spinning lure, or fly. This is state land extending nearly a half-mile upstream and about a mile downstream. Fishing pressure at Clark Bridge usually is light to moderate.

Site No. 6. Crocket Bridge

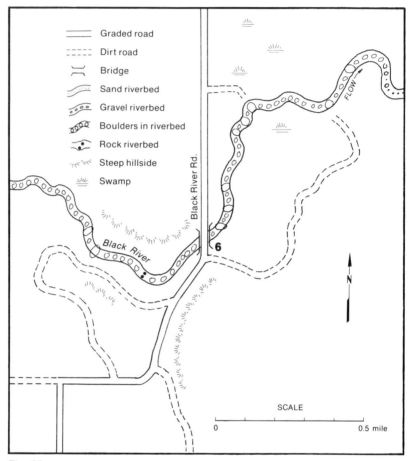

Fig. 66

Black River Road crosses the Black River at two bridges, one about 1.2 miles south of M-68 and one about 6.3 miles south of this highway. This is the south, or upstream bridge. The river is 60 to 80 feet wide and most of it is less than 4 feet deep. Some holes, like the one just below the bridge, will overtop your waders. The bottom is gravel and boulders. The flow is fast and the rocks are slippery, but the river can be waded here with caution at normal flows. At high flows the river is too deep and too fast for safe wading. The banks are low and mucky, forested with hardwood. Trout cover is sparse in this part of the river. State frontage extends upstream about 0.3 mile from this bridge. Downstream, the frontage is mostly private. Except for the early season, fishing pressure generally is light.

Site No. 7. Wigglesworth Road
Public Easement

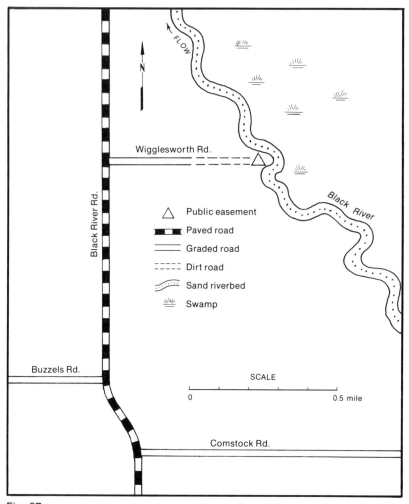

Wigglesworth Rd.

Black River Rd.

Black River

FLOW

N

△ Public easement

▰▰▰ Paved road

━━━ Graded road

- - - Dirt road

〰 Sand riverbed

≋ Swamp

Buzzels Rd.

SCALE

0   0.5 mile

Comstock Rd.

Fig. 67

There is parking space at the east end of Wigglesworth Road, but no other facilities at this site. This is one of several sites where the state holds an easement for public fishing along the stream banks. There is room to park two or three cars here and walk in about 100 feet to the river. The Black is 60 to 80 feet wide and 3 to 6 feet deep. Most of the river here is too deep for safe wading. The wading fisherman is likely to sink knee-deep into the soft sand and muck bottom. Most fishing is done from the banks or from a boat, using bait or spinning lures. The banks are generally low and swampy, lined with hardwood timber and brush. Except for the forty-acre easement, the banks are off limits to fishermen. Fishing pressure usually is light.

Boardman River

The Boardman is one of the best streams in Michigan for resident brown trout. It also has a good population of brook trout in the upper reaches and tributaries. Although trout are caught in the entire length of the river, the best all-season fishing is from the headwaters downstream to Brown Bridge Pond. This part of the river, including parts of the North and South Branches, was classified as Wild-Scenic in the Natural River Plan for the Boardman. A series of hydroelectric dams, most of them now inactive, prevent passage of steelhead and other anadromous fish into the upper river. Whether fish ladders should be installed to allow upstream migration of these fish is a controversial issue not yet resolved. Opponents argue that the migratory fish could spoil the excellent fishery for resident trout. The Natural River Plan for the Boardman recommends that the river system should be managed for the existing fish species, which would seem to exclude migratory fish.

The North Branch of the Boardman rises a few miles northeast of Kalkaska and flows generally southwest to join the South Branch about 7 miles south of the village of Williamsburg. The South Branch rises south of the village of South Boardman and flows northwest to its junction with the North Branch at "The Forks." Both branches provide good fishing, but the trout population of the South Branch is substantially greater than that of the North Branch.

From the Forks the Boardman flows generally southwest to Brown Bridge Pond, then west, northwest, and north to discharge into the west arm of Grand Traverse Bay. From the Forks downstream to Brown Bridge Pond, about 7 river miles, the Boardman is ideal fly water with an excellent population of brown trout and a fair population of brookies. Most of it has a firm gravel bottom, easy wading, and open enough for fly-fishing. More than half of the river frontage in this section is state land, providing ample access for fishermen.

Below Brown Bridge Dam almost all the frontage is private, and public access is sparse. This part of the river also provides good fishing, but it does not have the population of stream-bred trout that characterizes the upper river.

The Boardman is listed as one of the canoe trails in *Michigan Canoe Trails,* now out of print. Launching ramps are available at the campgrounds for canoes and other light boats. From the Forks to Brown Bridge Pond there are a few logjams and low bridges that require portages or lift overs. In the lower river portages are required around the dams. The Boardman above Brown Bridge Pond is too small and too fast for efficient boat fishing. Canoe traffic on the Boardman is relatively light, and fishermen on the river in the early morning or late evening are rarely bothered by canoes.

Like all good trout streams in the Midwest, the discharge of

The Boardman River at the Forks Campground

the Boardman is chiefly from groundwater, so the flow is relatively constant and the summer water temperatures are low. The Boardman is colder in the summer than the Au Sable, for example, but not quite so cold as the Manistee. The favorable water quality and abundant gravel spawning beds support natural reproduction sufficient to maintain the trout population here. Although the upper Boardman does not rise more than about 2 feet at high flows, this rise is enough to make most of the river unwadable. The flow of the Boardman generally is fast, much faster than that of the upper Au Sable, and wading in hip-deep water generally is not feasible. The river declines somewhat in dry periods, but generally not enough to seriously reduce trout cover.

Maps of the Boardman drafted in the early 1800s showed the Boardman as the Ottawa or "Ootawas" River, after the local Indians of that name (Melkild 1982). The present name is after a Captain Harry Boardman, who had his son build the first sawmill near the mouth of the Boardman River (Rayle 1982). In the early 1900s, the riverbanks were bleak and dismal with snags and slashings left over from the logging, according to Gordon Charles (1982). Nevertheless, the Boardman was considered one of the best in Michigan, first for grayling, then for trout. Charles tells of the Traverse City Fly Club organized by the late Art Winnie and nine of his cronies. The headquarters of the club, called "The Shack," was on the banks of the Boardman about 5 miles south of Traverse City.

Accommodations

Many motels and housekeeping cabins are available to fishermen at Kalkaska and Traverse City. For those who want to headquarter on the river, there are two state forest campgrounds and one resort-type motel on the upper Boardman. Ranch Rudolf, located on the Boardman between the Forks and Scheck's Place campgrounds, got its name from Rudolf Pazanier, chef and general manager of the Ranch Resort for many years (Melkild 1982). In the 1920s you could get, for $150.00 a week, "the use of a horse and buggy, lodging, and gourmet meals prepared by Rudolf himself." Excellent food still is served at Ranch Rudolf and there are many good restaurants in Traverse City and Kalkaska.

Although only 8 camping spaces are at the Forks Campground, spaces usually are available except on weekends. Scheck's Place Campground has space for 40 camping parties, and spaces usually are available here. For those who want more modern conveniences with their camping, Traverse City State Park offers 330 camping spaces on Grand Traverse Bay about 2 miles east of Traverse City.

Maps of the Boardman

Traverse City is a logical headquarters for fishing the Boardman, but the river can also be reached from the smaller towns of Kalkaska on the east and Kingsley on the south, or the little villages of Williamsburg on the north and South Boardman and Fife Lake on the southeast. The location map (fig. 68) shows the river channel and public roads leading to it.

Five numbered access sites are shown on this map, one on the North Branch, one on the South Branch, and three on the mainstream.

Use the Forks Bridge as the starting point for each of the sites. To get to Forks Bridge, go south out of the village of Williamsburg on the blacktop Williamsburg Road. About 5.7 miles south of Williamsburg you intersect with Supply Road coming in from the west. Continue south and southeast another 1.3 miles to Forks Bridge on the Boardman mainstream just below the junction of the North and South branches.

Site 1 (fig. 69) is on the North Branch at North Branch Bridge. Take a left turn on Supply Road just south of Forks Bridge and go east on this blacktop road about 0.3 mile to the intersection with a graded road turning off to the left (north). Turn left on this road, cross the South Branch, and continue north, east, and north again about 1.8 miles to North Branch Bridge.

Site 2 (fig. 70) is on the South Branch. Starting again at the Forks Bridge, turn left (east) on Supply Road and again go east on this road about 0.3 mile to the intersection with the graded road turning off to the left (north). Again, turn left (north) on this graded road and go about 0.2 mile to South Branch Bridge.

Site 3 (fig. 71) is the Forks Campground on the left (south) bank of the mainstream just below the Forks Bridge. Going south from Forks Bridge, turn right (west) on Brown Bridge Road, a graded road just south of Forks Bridge. Go west on this graded road

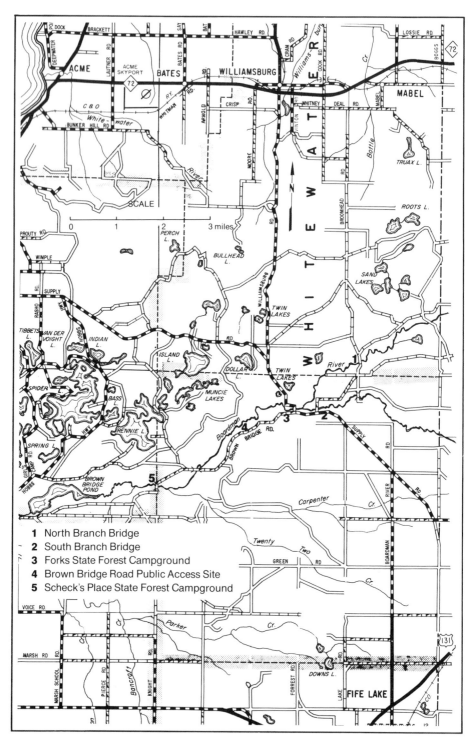

1 North Branch Bridge
2 South Branch Bridge
3 Forks State Forest Campground
4 Brown Bridge Road Public Access Site
5 Scheck's Place State Forest Campground

Fig. 68.   Location map of the Upper Boardman

about 0.3 mile to the campground entrance on the right (north) side of the road.

Site 4 (fig. 72) is an undeveloped public access site on state land about a mile southwest of the Forks Campground. Go southwest from the campground on Brown Bridge Road about 1.1 mile to a parking area on your right.

Site 5 (fig. 73) is Scheck's Place Campground. Continue southwest from site 4 on Brown Bridge Road. About 1.6 miles beyond site 4 you will cross a bridge at Ranch Rudolf. Continue west and southwest about 1 mile beyond this bridge to Scheck's Place Campground. The campground is just north of a bridge, the third bridge on the mainstream below the forks. A campground for horseback riders is about 0.5 mile upstream from here.

Site No. 1. North Branch Bridge

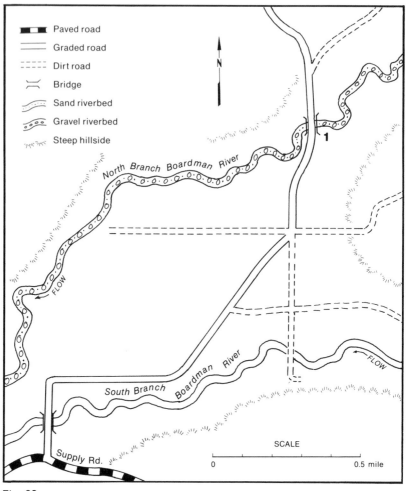

Paved road
Graded road
Dirt road
Bridge
Sand riverbed
Gravel riverbed
Steep hillside

N

North Branch Boardman River

FLOW

South Branch Boardman River

FLOW

Supply Rd.

SCALE

0   0.5 mile

1

Fig. 69

There is good off-road parking for several cars on the east side of the road just south of the bridge. The North Branch of the Boardman is 35 to 45 feet wide and 2 to 4 feet deep with some deeper holes. The hole just below the bridge, for example, is more than 6 feet deep. Bottom is sand and gravel with some muck. Banks are sandy, brushy, and forested with mixed hardwood and conifer. The river is wide enough for fly-fishing and deep enough for bait or spin fishing. Velocity is only moderate, and wading is fairly easy at normal flows if you watch out for the deeper holes, snags, and soft sand. The river frontage is mostly state land, but there are some private holdings, upstream and down. Fishing pressure usually is light. Population studies show the North Branch of the Boardman has more brown trout per unit area than the mainstream, but fewer brookies.

Site No. 2. South Branch Bridge

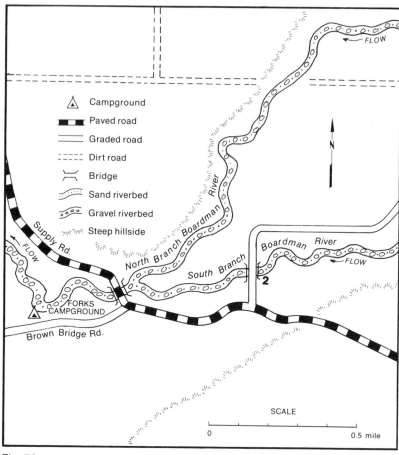

Legend
- Campground
- Paved road
- Graded road
- Dirt road
- Bridge
- Sand riverbed
- Gravel riverbed
- Steep hillside

FLOW

North Branch Boardman River

Boardman River

South Branch

FLOW

Supply Rd.

FLOW

FORKS CAMPGROUND

Brown Bridge Rd.

N

2

SCALE

0   0.5 mile

Fig. 70

There is very limited parking on the narrow shoulders here. One or two cars can park on the west side of the road just south of the bridge. Pull off as far as you can without going into the ditch so you are out of the traffic lane. It is a good idea to check the area on foot before you park. The South Branch of the Boardman is 30 to 40 feet wide here and averages about 3 feet deep. However, there are some holes that will overtop your waders. Bottom is gravel and sand with some muck. The banks are low, mucky, and brushy, with some open grassland at the riverside cabins. The velocity is moderate, and the river can be waded at normal flows if you avoid the deep holes. The river here can be fished with bait, spinning lures, or flies. The brushy banks make fly casting somewhat difficult but not impossible. Fishing pressure usually is light. The water is cooler here in summer than in the North Branch or mainstream, and trout populations are greater. The fall standing crop of brown trout, in weight per unit area, is more than double that of the North Branch, and nearly three times that of the mainstream (Gowing and Alexander 1980). There are few brookies in this water. Except for the road right-of-way, this is all private land.

Site No. 3. Forks State Forest Campground

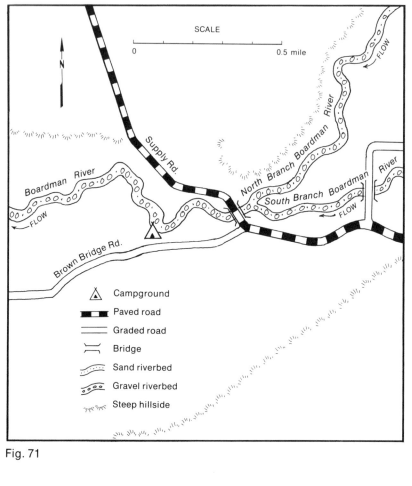

Fig. 71

This is one of the few state forest campgrounds that have not been moved back from the river's edge to protect the streambanks, probably because there is limited space between road and river here. The river frontage at the campground is state land, but there is private land on both banks upstream and down. The Forks is an attractive campground, equipped with water supply (well and hand pump), picnic tables, and outdoor toilets. It is an excellent headquarters for fishing the entire upper Boardman and both branches.

The river here is about 40 feet wide and averages about 2 feet deep at mid-channel. A few of the deeper holes will overtop your waders. The stream velocity is faster here than on the North and South branches, but wading is relatively easy at normal flows because of the generally shallower depth. The riverbed is mostly gravel, with some sand and a little muck. The banks are sandy, average about 4 feet high, and are forested with mixed conifers and hardwoods with considerable brush near the water's edge. The river is open and deep enough for all kinds of fishing.

Fishing pressure usually is light. Even when the campground is full you will usually find few of the campers on the river. If you fish early and late you have a good chance of having the river to yourself.

Site No. 4. Brown Bridge Road
Public Access Site

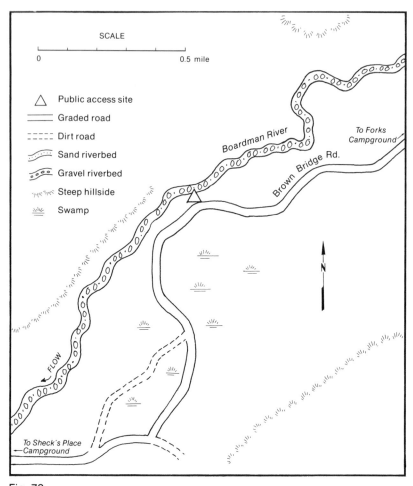

SCALE

0   0.5 mile

△ Public access site
═══ Graded road
- - - - Dirt road
Sand riverbed
Gravel riverbed
Steep hillside
Swamp

Boardman River

To Forks
Campground

Brown Bridge Rd.

N

FLOW

To Sheck's Place
Campground

Fig. 72

Brown Bridge Road parallels the Boardman River on the south from the Forks Campground downstream (southwest) to the bridge at Ranch Rudolf. The road comes very close to the river about 1 mile downstream from the campground, and there are three parking areas between the road and river in the next 0.4 mile.

The river is 40 to 50 feet wide here and 1 to 4 feet deep, with some deeper holes that will overtop your waders. The bottom is sand and gravel. The flow is fast, much faster than in the flies-only water of the Au Sable, for example, but the river can be waded with care if you avoid the deeper runs. At high flows the river here is mostly unwadable. The banks on the south side are about 5 feet high, mostly low and swampy on the north. There is considerable brush at the river's edge, backed by white and red pine and mixed hardwoods. Access to the river is easy, but tread softly on the sandy banks. This is all state land for about a mile downstream, but there is private property upstream. Fishing pressure here usually is light to moderate. There are large brown trout in this area and good hatches of large mayflies here and downstream.

Site No. 5. Scheck's Place State Forest Campground

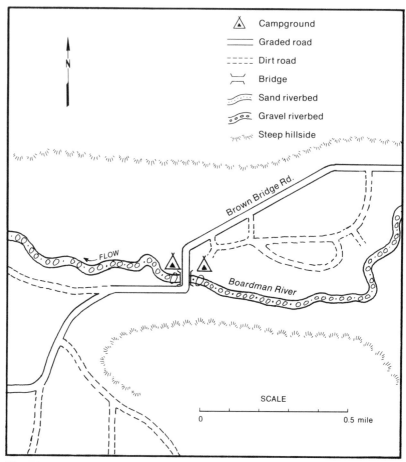

Fig. 73

Brown Bridge Road turns south to cross the Boardman here, and the campground is on both sides of the road on the right (north) bank of the river. The Boardman is about 50 feet wide here and averages about 2 feet deep at mid-channel at normal flows. There are some shallow riffles and some holes that will overtop your waders. The streambed is mostly gravel and boulders, with some sand and muck. The velocity of flow is fast, but the stream can be waded with care at normal flows. The banks are mostly low, 1 to 5 feet high, and very brushy, with some large white pine, smaller red pine, and poplar. Overhanging brush and snags provide good cover.

State land extends from the bridge upstream about a half-mile and downstream about one-quarter mile. You can launch a canoe at the campground and fish on down to Brown Bridge Pond, about 2 river miles. Fishing pressure usually is light to moderate.

Rifle River

The Rifle River in Ogemaw County is one of the few good trout streams in the eastern part of Michigan's Lower Peninsula. The Rifle is best known as a brown trout fishery, but in recent years it has become popular with steelhead and chinook salmon fishermen. The best water for resident trout is the mainstream above Selkirk and in some of the tributaries to the upper river. The mainstream from its source near the west end of Devoe Lake downstream to the village of Selkirk is mostly shallow enough for wading and wide enough for all kinds of fishing. The tributaries to the upper river are generally too narrow and brushy for easy fly casting.

The population of resident trout in the Rifle, almost exclusively brown trout, is lower than most other streams considered here. Nevertheless, the Rifle yields good catches to early season fishermen, especially bait and spin fishermen. Later in the season, when fishing tapers off, the fly-fisherman may often have the stream all to himself.

The glacial deposits and the soils derived from them in the Rifle River basin are not so sandy as those of the rivers to the north and west. A smaller amount of the snowmelt and rainfall soaks into the ground, and more runs over the surface to the stream. Consequently, the Rifle rises rather quickly and becomes quite cloudy after heavy rains, even in midsummer. Wading becomes more difficult then, because the flow becomes swifter, and the murky water hides the holes that may overtop your waders.

Devoe Lake, about 4 miles southeast of Rose City, formerly was the source of the Rifle. In the early 1950s, a diversion was constructed around the lake to allow the relatively cold water from Gamble Creek and its tributaries to flow directly into the Rifle. From the west end of Devoe Lake downstream to Sage Lake Road (about 4.5 river miles) the river is in the Rifle River Recreation Area. All river frontage here is state land.

From Sage Lake Road (also called County 18) downstream to a half-mile north of Selkirk (about 4.8 river miles) the Rifle is in the Au Sable State Forest. About two-thirds of the frontage in the state forest is state land. The rest is private.

Some of the tributaries to the upper Rifle also provide good fishing. Both Houghton and Gamble creeks have trout populations substantially greater than the mainstream for comparable area. Houghton Creek, the largest of the tributaries, is more than 30 feet wide in places below the junction with Wilkins Creek, but much of it is too deep for wading. Gamble Creek is shallower, but too narrow and brushy for most fly fishermen.

Canoe traffic on the Rifle is increasing, especially with Scouts and other youth groups. When you see the first of one of these groups you might as well rest on the bank until they all go by. If you are on the river in the early morning or late evening you will not usually be bothered by canoes.

The Rifle River at the Rifle River Campground

The Rifle has been designated a Natural River by the DNR. The cultivated fields and many paved roads in this area are hardly conducive to a wilderness atmosphere. However, the Rifle River area has a pastoral beauty that is quite appealing. The hardwood forest in the Rifle River Recreation Area and in the Au Sable State Forest are especially attractive in the early spring with the delicate pinks, yellows, and greens of the budding leaves, and again, when the trees are in full color in the fall.

Early residents of the Rifle River area were the Indians whose earthwork remnants may still be seen near the river north of Selkirk. No doubt they used the river to supply fish and as a means of transportation. The Indians were followed by fur traders and, later, the lumbermen who harvested most of the timber in the area. Some of the lumbermen stayed on to become farmers, and farming remains an important industry in the area to this day. With the cutting of the forests and the farming that followed, the land was exposed to erosion. Much effort has been made in the Rifle watershed to control this problem, but it has not yet been entirely resolved. The Natural River Plan by the DNR includes recommendations for erosion control in the Rifle River area.

Another problem on the Rifle not common to most of the trout streams to the north and west is flooding. In late May of 1959 an intense storm dropped about 4 inches of rain on the upper Rifle watershed in about 6 hours, causing the Rifle to overflow its banks. Bridges and culverts and sections of roads were washed away. Damage to roads in Ogemaw County was estimated to be more than $100,000. Floods of this magnitude are very rare, but the Rifle rises faster and higher than most good trout streams in the northern part of Michigan's Lower Peninsula.

Although the flow of the Rifle is more variable than that of most other rivers described here, the river has a strong drought flow, maintained in part by groundwater flow from adjacent basins to the north and west. This groundwater inflow helps to keep the river cool in summer, and the summer water temperatures are similar to those on the flies-only water of the Au Sable. The water in the Rifle is hard, moderately alkaline, and generally of suitable quality for trout. Gravel for spawning beds is somewhat sparse in the Rifle River Recreation Area but appears adequate from here downstream to Selkirk.

Accommodations

Rose City has several good motels and restaurants. Advance reservations may be needed during the summer season. Fishing tackle is available at several stores in Rose City, but the supply of trout flies is quite limited.

Four camping areas are in the Rifle River Recreation Area, with space for about 150 camping parties. One of these, located on the north side of Grousehaven Lake, has all modern facilities. One rustic campground is on the south side of Devoe Lake and two are on the banks of the Rifle. The rustic campgrounds are equipped with box toilets and hand pumps. These campgrounds may be crowded, especially in the summertime, but few of the campers do much fishing on the Rifle.

If all the spaces in the recreation area are filled, you can usually find space available in the Rifle River Campground to the south. This is a rustic campground, with outdoor toilets, a hand pump, and a flowing well. There is space for forty camping parties here.

Maps of the Rifle

The location map (fig. 74) shows the Rifle River from its source to the village of Selkirk. All public roads leading to the river and five numbered access sites are also shown on this map.

The Rifle River Recreation Area (site 1, fig. 75) is about 5 miles east of Rose City. Take Rose City Road (County 22) east out of Rose City. Exactly 4.5 miles east of the center of Rose City you will come to the intersection with Lupton Road leading off to the left (north) toward Lupton. Continue about 0.2 mile beyond this intersection to the park entrance on the right (south). Stop at the park office and pay an entrance fee if you do not have an annual permit. The park officials will give you a map showing the roads leading to the river and the four campgrounds in the area. The shortest way to the river is by way of Ranch Road leading off to the right from the entrance road and circling Grousehaven Lake and Mallard Pond on the left (south and east) of the road. You will cross several creeks before you come to the Rifle River just west of Devoe Lake.

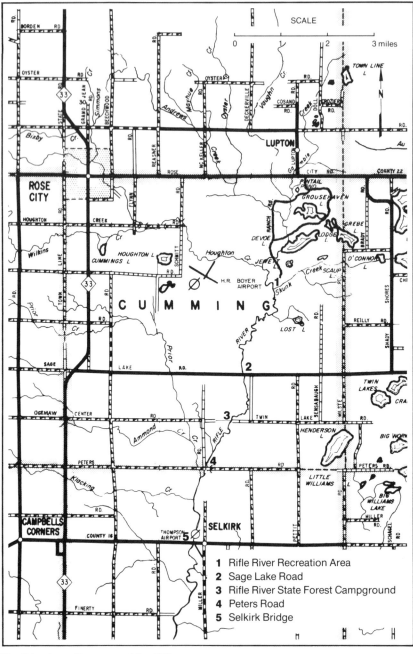

Fig. 74.   Location map of the Rifle

1 Rifle River Recreation Area
2 Sage Lake Road
3 Rifle River State Forest Campground
4 Peters Road
5 Selkirk Bridge

Sage Lake Road (site 2, fig. 76) crosses the Rifle about 5 miles southeast of Rose City. Drive south out of Rose City on M-33 about 4.2 miles to the intersection with Sage Lake Road (County 18). Turn left (east) on Sage Lake Road and go 3.4 miles to the bridge.

Rifle River Campground (site 3, fig. 77) is 1 mile south of Sage Lake Road. Continue east on Sage Lake Road about 1.2 miles past the bridge on the Rifle (site 2) to an improved road leading off to the right (south). Take this road south just 1 mile to Twin Lake Road. Turn right again (west) on Twin Lake Road and go 1.3 miles to the campground.

Peters Road is just 2 miles south of Sage Lake Road. To get to the bridge on Peters Road (site 4, fig. 78), take M-33 south out of Rose City about 6.3 miles to the intersection with Peters Road. Turn left (east) on Peters Road and go about 3 miles to the bridge.

Selkirk Bridge (site 5, fig. 79) is 1.5 miles south of Peters Road Bridge. Go south out of Rose City on M-33 about 7.8 miles to the intersection with County 16. Turn left (east) on the county road and go about 2.7 miles to the bridge.

Site No. 1. Rifle River
Recreation Area

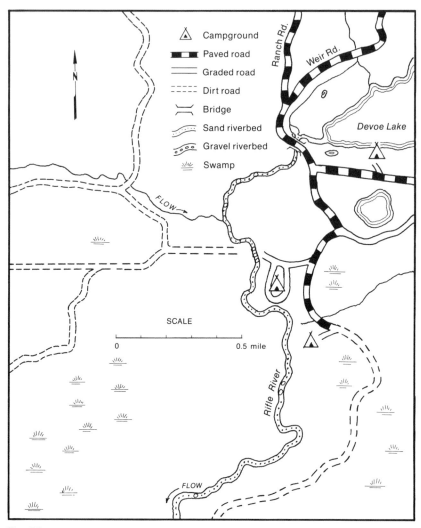

Campground
Paved road
Graded road
Dirt road
Bridge
Sand riverbed
Gravel riverbed
Swamp

N

Ranch Rd.

Weir Rd.

Devoe Lake

FLOW

SCALE

0   0.5 mile

Rifle River

FLOW

Fig. 75

There is easy access to the Rifle at several points within the Rifle River Recreation Area. Two of the rustic campgrounds south of Devoe Lake are handy to the river, and Rifle River Road follows the river downstream (south) on the east side to a turnaround near the southern boundary of the area.

The Rifle is 40 to 50 feet wide in this area and open enough for all kinds of fishing. Depth of channel is extremely variable, ranging from less than 1 foot in some of the gravel riffles to more than 5 feet in some of the deeper holes. Bottom material is sand, gravel, and muck, with sand predominating. The banks are low and brushy, with hardwood and conifer forest and some open grassy areas. Wading is fairly easy at normal flows if you watch out for the deeper holes. Be especially careful when the water is murky. At very high flows the river is unwadable. Some parts of the river are open enough to fish from the banks.

This is very attractive water and a pleasant place to fish. You can fish downstream all the way to Sage Lake Road without fear of trespassing on private property. Fishing pressure is moderate to heavy in the early season. In the late season, and especially in the early morning or late evening, you may be able to find reaches of the river where you can fish alone.

The lands now making up the Rifle River Recreation Area were formerly owned by the late Harry M. Jewett, one of the earliest auto manufacturers (Vandemark 1975). In the 1920s he built a private hunting and fishing retreat here he called "Grousehaven." Jewett was greatly concerned with the restoration of wild game and fish populations in the area. He raised trout and introduced them into his own waters and also into other local streams. After his death in 1937, the Jewett family showed little interest in Grousehaven, and the property, some 4,300 acres, was purchased by the Michigan Department of Conservation. It is now a state park.

Site No. 2. Sage Lake Road

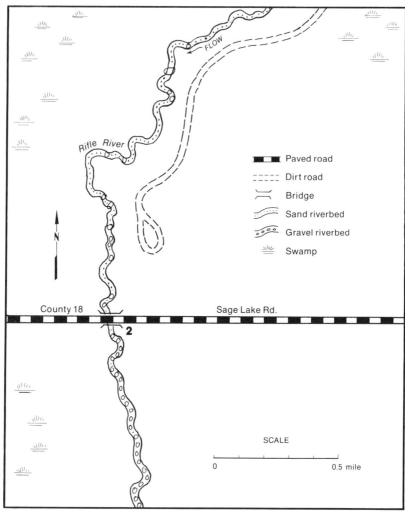

Fig. 76

Sage Lake Road (County 18) is the boundary between the Rifle River Recreation Area on the north (upstream) and the Au Sable State Forest (formerly the Ogemaw State Forest) to the south. All the riverbanks upstream are state land, but some of the downstream frontage is private. The river here is 40 to 60 feet wide and 1 to 3 feet deep, with some deeper holes. The bottom material is mostly sand upstream. Downstream, the bottom is chiefly gravel, with several gravel riffles. The banks are low and brushy for the most part, but there are some high banks and some open grassy areas. Wading is generally easy at normal flows. At high flows wading may be difficult to dangerous. The water is clear at normal flows but turns cloudy rather quickly after heavy rains. The river is open enough for all kinds of fishing, including bank fishing in the grassy areas. Fishing pressure is moderate except during the steelhead runs. This is the upstream limit for the extended season for steelhead. Brown trout may not be taken during the extended season on the Rifle.

Site No. 3. Rifle River State Forest Campground

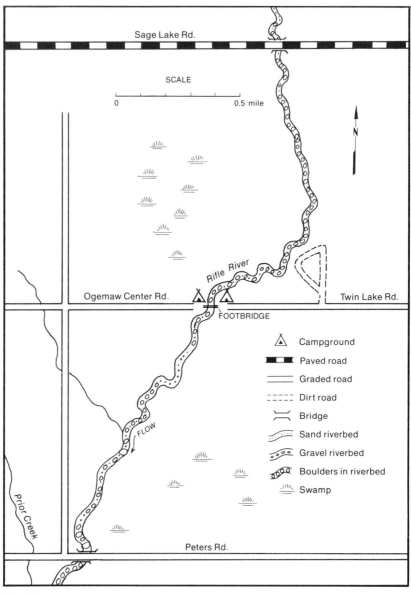

Sage Lake Rd.

SCALE

0   0.5 mile

N

Rifle River

Ogemaw Center Rd.

Twin Lake Rd.

FOOTBRIDGE

FLOW

Prior Creek

Peters Rd.

△   Campground

▮▮▮   Paved road

Graded road

Dirt road

⊃⊂   Bridge

Sand riverbed

Gravel riverbed

Boulders in riverbed

Swamp

Fig. 77

218 • Rifle River

This is an attractive campground, with spaces on both sides of the river, connected by a footbridge. There is a hand pump on the east side of the river and a flowing well on the west side. The campground usually is not crowded, but groups of canoeists occasionally stop overnight here and may take up most of the available spaces.

The river is about 40 feet wide here and mostly 2 to 3 feet deep, with some holes that will overtop your waders. The river bottom is sand and gravel with some patches of clay. Banks are low and brushy. Wading is fairly easy at low flows if you watch out for the deeper holes. At high flows, wading may be impossible. The river can be fished with bait, spinner, or fly, although the brushy banks may be troublesome to the fly-fisherman. There are some large fish in the deeper holes in this part of the river. Even when the campground is full, you will usually find few other fishermen on the river here.

Site No. 4. Peters Road

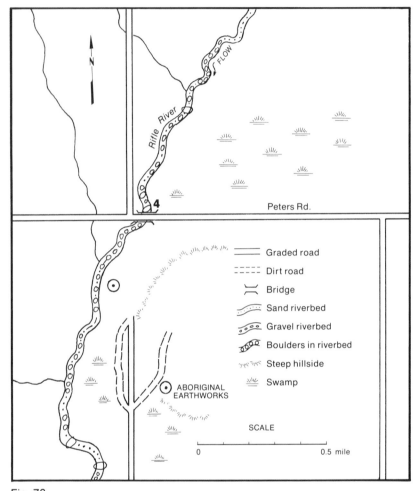

Fig. 78

This site is within the boundaries of the Au Sable State Forest, but most of the frontage is private. There is some state land right at the bridge. There is room to park two to three cars on the south side of the road west of the bridge. The river is 40 to 50 feet wide here and 1 to 3 feet deep with a few deeper holes. The river bottom is mostly gravel and boulders. The flow is swift and the rocks are slippery, but the river can be waded with care at normal flows. At high flows wading is impossible. The banks are low and mucky, lined with brush and hardwood. The river is open enough for all kinds of fishing. Fishing pressure may be heavy during steelhead runs, but it is light most of the rest of the season.

Site No. 5. Selkirk Bridge

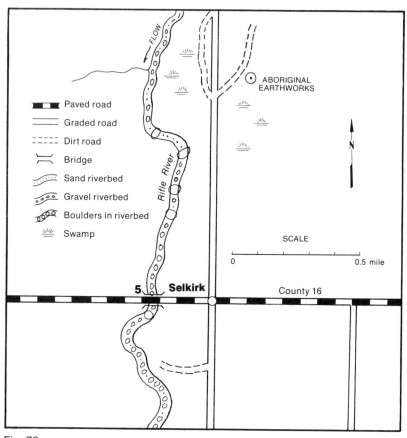

FLOW

ABORIGINAL
EARTHWORKS

Rifle River

Paved road
Graded road
Dirt road
Bridge
Sand riverbed
Gravel riverbed
Boulders in riverbed
Swamp

N

SCALE

0   0.5 mile

5   Selkirk   County 16

Fig. 79

This is all private land except for the road right-of-way. Parking is not permitted near the bridge. However, fishermen can obtain permission from Carscallen's Canoe Rental at Selkirk to park at their canoe landing on the south side of the road just west of the bridge. Check in at the store just west of the landing. The Rifle is about 60 feet wide here and generally less than 4 feet deep, with some deeper holes. The river bottom is gravel and boulders with some sand. The river can be waded at normal flows, but wading is never easy. The flow is swift, and the cobbles and boulders do not provide a stable footing. Felt-soled boots would be a help in this water. At high flows the river here is unwadable. Banks are generally low and mucky. Trout cover is sparse. Fishing pressure may be heavy during steelhead runs, but usually is light the rest of the season.

Pere Marquette River

The Pere Marquette, one of Michigan's classic trout streams, is famous for its large brown and steelhead trout. A beautiful, unspoiled river, the Pere Marquette has been classified as a National Scenic River by the U.S. Forest Service. It has also been designated a Natural River by the state of Michigan. The Pere Marquette country is not a wilderness area, but the hardwood forests, rolling hills, and many lakes are most attractive. This is one of the few larger rivers that flows free of impoundments from the headwaters all the way to Lake Michigan. In recent years the Pere Marquette has had heavy fall runs of Pacific salmon, but this is not considered an unmixed blessing by those who prefer fishing the resident trout. The competition of the salmon for spawning beds caused a decline in the brown trout fishery. Some browns have been planted in the Pere Marquette since 1989, and the resident fishery has improved somewhat. In 1977 and subsequent years Atlantic salmon were also planted in the Pere Marquette, but these plantings have not been successful.

From its headwaters near the village of Chase, the Pere Marquette flows westward about 75 river miles to the mouth at Ludington. It is a small stream above Idlewild, best suited for bait fishing. It is joined by the Little South Branch southeast of Baldwin, and from here all the way to Ludington it is wide enough and open enough for all kinds of fishing. The river from the M-37 Bridge downstream to Gleason's Landing, about 7 river miles, is restricted to fly-fishing, but the rest of the river is open to bait and spin fishing also.

The Pere Marquette does not have the miles of easy wading found on some Michigan rivers, the Au Sable for example, but much of the river from the mouth of the Little South Branch downstream to a few miles below Bowman Bridge (about 12 river miles) can be waded with caution at normal flows. Most of the river below that point is too deep and fast for easy wading, and much of the fishing is done from boats or by wading near the banks.

The river can be floated by canoe or other light boat all the way from the Forks above Baldwin to the mouth. Amateur boaters may have problems at Rainbow Rapids, and some authorities recommend that the novice should not try to run these. Yet I have seen many a rank amateur go through these rapids with no more damage than a few bumps on the rocks. The two reaches of braided stream, one between Walhalla and Custer, and one just below Scottville, may slow you up a bit, but with a little time and patience you can find the through channel. The Pere Marquette is a meandering stream, and in some reaches you will go 2 or more miles along the meanders for every cross-country mile downstream. On a windy day you will be bucking a head wind at times, and at others the wind will be at your back, helping you along. Several boat-launching and pickup sites are on the river.

The Pere Marquette River above Gleason's Landing

Some of the existing public access sites and campgrounds on the river may be discontinued in the future and some new ones may be developed, according to the U.S. Forest Service Management Plan. The access at Green Cottage, for example, about 1.5 miles west of M-37 Bridge, may be closed if a better access can be established nearby. Rainbow Rapids access, between Bowman Bridge and Sulak, also may be closed when a new site is acquired. All the sites described in this guide are scheduled for continuing maintenance, although the rules governing their use may change.

The Middle Branch of the Pere Marquette rises in the morainal hills that form the eastern boundary of the drainage basin. West of this morainal area the river flows across a broad plain of sand and gravel that extends westward to Custer. The river crosses another belt of moraine between Custer and Scottville and then crosses a sandy lake plain to the mouth at Ludington. It is the broad plain of sand and gravel between the headwaters and Custer that contributes most of the groundwater to maintain the flow of cool water during the hot summer months.

Although the Pere Marquette is a relatively stable stream, it rises and falls 3 to 4 feet in a normal year. Because much of the river is only marginally wadable at low flows, high water on the Pere Marquette makes most of the river unwadable. The velocity of flow on the Pere Marquette ranges from less than 1 foot per second in the pools to more than 5 feet per second at Rainbow Rapids. It is the velocity as well as the depth that makes much of the river unwadable.

The quality of water in the Pere Marquette is excellent for trout. The water is hard, moderately alkaline, and the temperature of the water rarely goes much above 70 degrees F, even on the hottest summer days. The excellent quality of water and the extensive gravel spawning beds in the upper river make the Pere Marquette almost ideal trout habitat.

The Pere Marquette has been famous for its trout fishing for nearly a century, but trout were not native to this river. An article in the *Lake County Star* by Don Ingle (1973) listed the menominee (a whitefish), the grayling, and the sucker as the native fish in the Pere Marquette. Of these, only the sucker remains in the river. The Michigan grayling is now extinct, and the whitefish is no longer caught in the Pere Marquette.

One of the oldest fishing clubs in the area, the "Pere

Marquette Fishing Club," was located on Kinney Creek, about 5 miles west of Baldwin. An article in the *Detroit Free Press* (August 23, 1892) assured its readers:

> The public can rest assured that the action of the new owners of Kinne Creek will not detract from the pleasures which fishermen have enjoyed heretofore in that vicinity. It is sure that one stream will be closed to the public, but the benefit that adjoining streams will receive from the planting of brook trout, lake trout, German trout and bass in the adjoining waters will more than compensate them.

A prime developer of "fishing clubs" on the river, according to Mr. George F. Dechow (personal communication 1983), was the Pere Marquette Railroad, originally the Chicago and West Michigan Railroad. The *Northern Michigan Handbook for Travelers* (Inglis 1898) refers to the clubhouse on the river south of Baldwin and states that "This is a well known trout stream where the beautiful 'rainbow' trout are found." It appears that all three trouts—brooks, brown, and rainbows—were fished in the Pere Marquette by the late 1800s.

Accommodations

Many motels, cabins, and restaurants in Baldwin and other towns and villages along the river are eager to serve the fishermen. The city of Ludington at the mouth of the river has a wide variety of accommodations.

Two campgrounds are on the river between Baldwin and the village of Branch. These are maintained by the U.S. Forest Service. A third campground is maintained by the town of Scottville on the lower river. Other campgrounds, near but not on the river, include Ludington State Park north of Ludington, Timber Creek Campground maintained by the U.S. Forest Service north of U.S. 10 near Branch, and Bray Creek and Little Leverentz state forest campgrounds northeast of Baldwin.

Fishing tackle and other supplies of all kinds can be obtained at Baldwin, Custer, Scottville, and Ludington. Canoes can be rented in Baldwin.

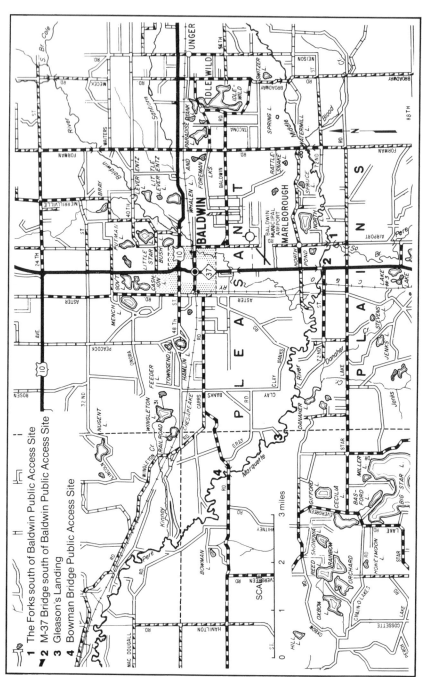

H H H

1 The Forks south of Baldwin Public Access Site
2 M-37 Bridge south of Baldwin Public Access Site
3 Gleason's Landing
4 Bowman Bridge Public Access Site

Fig. 80. Location map of the Pere Marquette, headwaters to Bowman Bridge Public Access Site

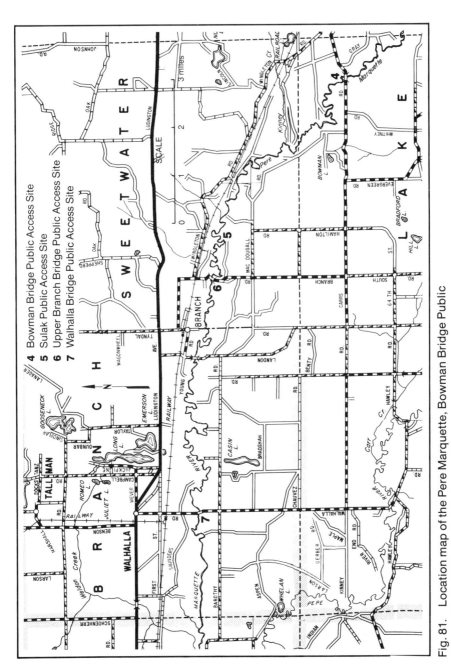

Fig. 81. Location map of the Pere Marquette, Bowman Bridge Public Access Site to Walhalla Public Access Site

4 Bowman Bridge Public Access Site
5 Sulak Public Access Site
6 Upper Branch Bridge Public Access Site
7 Walhalla Bridge Public Access Site

Maps of the Pere Marquette

The channel of the Pere Marquette and public roads leading to the river are shown on the location maps (figs. 80 and 81). Five bridges cross the river between Baldwin and Walhalla. Several other roads reach, but do not cross, the river. Most of the roads in the area run north-south or east-west along section lines, so it is easy to find your way to the desired location. Seven public access sites are shown on the location maps.

To get to site 1 (fig. 82), take M-37 south out of Baldwin. You will cross the bridge over the Pere Marquette about 2.75 miles south of the center of town. Continue south past this bridge 0.5 mile, then turn left (east) and go east 0.5 mile to a north-south road. You will cross a bridge over the Little South Branch of the Pere Marquette about 0.1 mile before you get to the north-south road. Turn left again (north) on this road and go about 0.2 mile north to the public access site on the left (west) side of the road.

Site 2 (fig. 83) is on the south bank of the river just upstream from the bridge on M-37. Go south out of Baldwin on M-37 2.75 miles to the road on the left just past the bridge. Turn left (east) on this road into the access site.

Gleason's Landing (site 3, fig. 84) is about 2.5 river miles upstream from Bowman Bridge. Go west out of Baldwin on Carrs Road exactly 2 miles from the west edge of town to the intersection with a graded road turning off to the left (south). There is a sign "Gleasons" at the turnoff. Turn left here and go 0.5 mile to a fork in the road. Take the right fork and go southwest 0.7 mile to the intersection with an east-west road coming in from the left. Turn right (west) here and go 0.4 mile to the intersection with another road leading off to the left (south). Turn left on this road and go 0.5 mile to a fork in the road. Take the right fork and go 0.1 mile to the parking area near the campground. A path leads from the parking lot about 100 yards to the river.

Site 4 (fig. 85) is just downstream from Bowman Bridge. Go west and southwest out of Baldwin on Carrs Road about 4.5 miles to the bridge. Cross the bridge and turn right (north) about 0.1 mile past the bridge.

Site 5 (fig. 86) is upstream from Upper Branch Bridge. Take the South Branch Road out of the village of Branch and go south from U.S. 10 0.5 mile, then east 1 mile, then south again 0.6 mile to the Upper Branch Bridge. Continue generally south about 0.6 mile beyond the bridge to a dirt road leading off to the left. Take a hard left turn onto this road and go north about 0.2 mile. Here the road turns east. Follow the road as it winds east and northeast about 0.8 mile to the access site.

Site 6 (fig. 87) is just downstream from Upper Branch Bridge. Starting again at the village of Branch, go south and east and south again on the South Branch Road 2.1 miles to the Upper Branch Bridge. Turn right (west) just past the bridge into the access site.

Site 7 (fig. 88) is on the south bank of the Pere Marquette just downstream from Walhalla Bridge. From the intersection of U.S. 10 and Walhalla Road in Walhalla, go south on Walhalla Road 1.4 miles to Walhalla Bridge. Cross the bridge and turn right (west) into the public access site.

Site No. 1. The Forks South of Baldwin Public Access Site

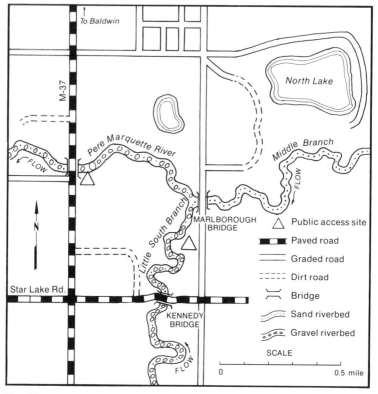

Fig. 82

This public access on the Little South Branch of the Pere Marquette has parking space for about twenty cars. The river is about 35 feet wide here and 2 to 3 feet deep, with some deeper holes. It is shallow enough for wading at normal flows and open enough for fly-fishing. The bottom is mostly gravel, with some sand. The banks are low and sandy, brushy in places, and partly forested with hardwoods and conifers. This is a major canoe-launching site, so fishermen should park their cars well back from the launching area. Population studies by the DNR showed about 70 pounds of trout per acre in this water. Fishing pressure usually is light to moderate. Some large brown trout are in this water.

Site No. 2. M-37 Bridge South of Baldwin Public Access Site

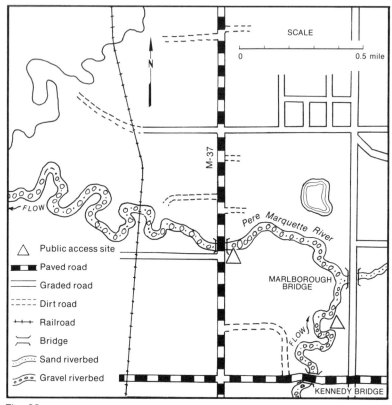

SCALE

0   0.5 mile

N

M-37

FLOW

Pere Marquette River

△ Public access site
■■■ Paved road
—— Graded road
----- Dirt road
+++++ Railroad
⋈ Bridge
~~~ Sand riverbed
∘∘∘ Gravel riverbed

MARLBOROUGH BRIDGE

FLOW

KENNEDY BRIDGE

Fig. 83

The flies-only water on the Pere Marquette begins at the M-37 Bridge and extends downstream to Gleason's Landing (about 7 river miles). Creel limit is now (1993) one trout or salmon over 16 inches. For many trout fishermen, this size restriction is almost equivalent to a no-kill regulation. Standard regulations apply upstream from the bridge. The public access site is on the south bank of the river just upstream (east) of the bridge. There is parking space for about twenty-five cars. The river here is about 60 feet wide and 2 to 4 feet deep, with some deeper holes. The bottom material is gravel and sand with a few boulders. The banks upstream from the bridge are low and lined with brush and hardwoods. Downstream from the bridge the north bank is high and sandy. The river can be waded with care at normal flows and is wide enough for easy fly casting. There are some large browns in this water. Population studies a short distance downstream from the bridge showed 90 pounds of trout per acre. Fishing pressure is heavy during the spring and fall spawning runs, but is generally light at mid-season.

This is also a popular boat-launching site, so fishermen should keep well back from the ramp. The site is equipped with toilets. Camping is no longer permitted here. Except for the public access site, this is all private land.

Site No. 3. Gleason's Landing

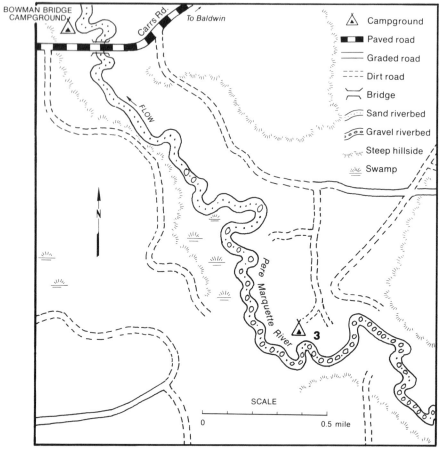

Fig. 84

This is the downstream limit of the flies-only water. Parking is available for about twelve cars. You will have to walk in about 100 yards to the river. Camping is permitted here, and a water pump, toilets, and picnic tables are provided. The river here is 3 to 6 feet deep and 70 to 80 feet wide. Parts of it can be waded with care at normal flows, but you will overtop your waders at mid-channel in many places. The velocity is moderate to fast, so wading is never easy. The bottom is sand and gravel. The banks are low, forested with hardwoods. The river is wide and open enough for easy fly casting. This is a favorite spot with many steelhead fishermen, because they have the choice of fishing upstream in the flies-only water or downstream, where other methods are permitted. Fishing pressure is heavy during the spawning runs, but is generally moderate the rest of the season. Most of the river frontage downstream is federal land, but there are some private holdings. Upstream, most of the land is private.

Site No. 4. Bowman Bridge Public Access Site

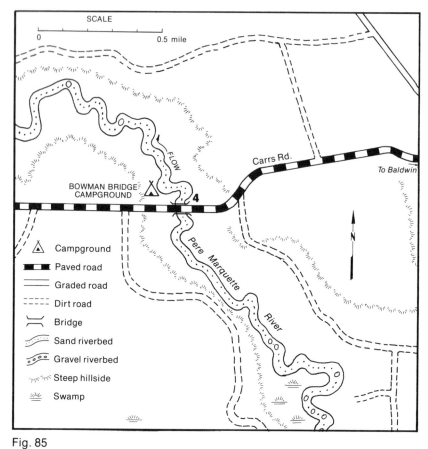

Fig. 85

This public access site is maintained by the National Forest Service. It has parking space for forty-eight cars and has a new campground with room for sixteen camping parties. The campground is on the left bank of the river just downstream from the bridge. The camp has drinking water and vault toilets.

The river is about 70 to 80 feet wide here. Bottom is chiefly sand with some gravel. Upstream from the bridge, the river is 3 to 6 feet deep. Downstream, it is generally less than 4 feet deep, with some deeper holes. Wading downstream from the bridge is possible at normal flows if you avoid the deeper parts. Upstream, wading is difficult to impossible. Banks are mostly low downstream, a little higher upstream, forested with hardwoods. The banks are mostly federal land, but there are some private holdings. Fishing pressure here is generally moderate except during the spring and fall spawning runs.

Site No. 5. Sulak Public Access Site

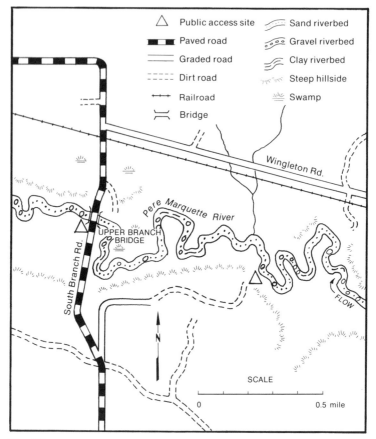

Fig. 86

This public access site southeast of Branch is maintained by the DNR. It has parking space for about fifty cars and is heavily used by canoeists and fishermen. The site is equipped with an outdoor toilet and trash containers. Camping is not permitted at this site, but a campground may be developed here in the future.

The Pere Marquette is about 60 feet wide here and 3 to 6 feet deep. It is generally too deep and fast for safe wading at mid-channel, but some parts can be waded with care along the banks. Bottom is sand, gravel, and clay. The riverbanks are alternately high and low, more than 20 feet high in places, and forested with hardwoods. The river here is heavily fished in the spring and fall spawning runs, but is moderate to light the rest of the season.

Site No. 6. Upper Branch Bridge
Public Access Site

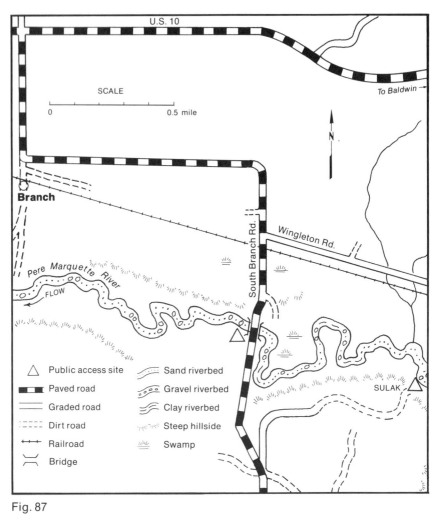

Fig. 87

This public access site just downstream from the bridge is maintained by the National Forest Service. It has room to park about thirty cars and is equipped with toilets, well, picnic tables, and fire grates. Camping has been permitted here but will be prohibited in the future, and the picnic tables and fire grates will be removed.

The river is 50 to 60 feet wide here and 3 to 6 feet deep. The bottom material is sand, gravel, and clay. The river is generally too deep and fast for wading, even at low flows. Most fishing is done by boat. Canoes and other boats can be launched and landed here. River frontage downstream from the bridge is mostly federal land. Upstream, most frontage is private. The riverbanks are alternately high and low, forested with hardwood. Fishing pressure usually is light except during spawning runs.

Site No. 7. Walhalla Bridge Public Access Site

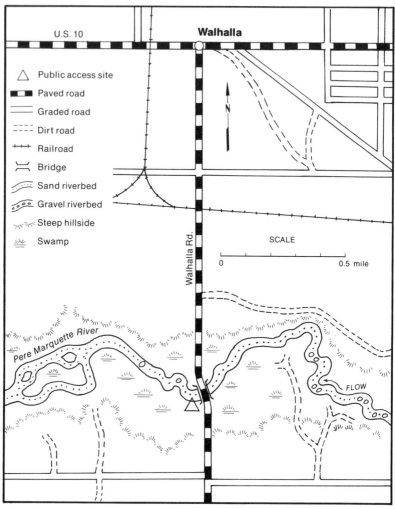

Fig. 88

This public access site is maintained by the state. The site has room for about twelve cars and provides toilets and trash containers. This is a major access for canoeists and fishermen.

The river is 60 to 70 feet wide and 3 to 6 feet deep. Bottom is mostly sand, with some gravel. The river is mostly too deep and swift for safe wading at mid-channel. Most fishing here is done from boats. Canoes and other light boats can be launched and landed here. This part of the river usually is not heavily fished, except during the spring and fall spawning runs. The riverbanks are state land downstream from the bridge. Upstream, there is some state land, but most is private.

Pine River

The Pine is a top-quality trout stream flowing through mostly hardwood forest south and west of Cadillac to the backwaters of Tippy Dam. It has a good population of rainbows and browns, with some brook trout in the upper reaches. Several hundred adult spring-run steelhead from the Little Manistee River were transferred to the Pine during the period 1973 to 1975, but no trout have been planted in the Pine for several years, and all rainbows now caught are stream-bred. Steelhead are blocked from entering the Pine by Tippy Dam, and all rainbows in the Pine are resident fish. The Pine has been designated one of Michigan's Blue Ribbon Trout Streams. It is one of Michigan's best streams for resident rainbows.

The river remains relatively wild, with few riverfront cabins or other developments. A scattering of conifers among the hardwoods gives a pleasing variety to the forest cover. The Pine is lightly fished. It never undergoes the fishing pressure of more popular streams such as the Au Sable system. Although canoe traffic is likely to be heavy on summer weekends, traffic is generally lighter during the week. No canoes are allowed on the river in the early morning or late evening. The fisherman who likes solitude while fishing should enjoy the Pine.

Probably one reason the fishing pressure is light is that the Pine is generally a difficult river to fish with a fly. From the headwaters to below Peterson Bridge on M-37, the Pine flows fast and fairly deep, and is never easy to wade, even at low water. At high flows, the Pine is almost entirely unwadable. The average depth at normal summer flows probably is slightly less than 3 feet, but this figure can be misleading. At mid-channel, the stream is mostly more than 3 feet deep, and is well over your waders in many places.

Another hazard to waders on the Pine is the hard, consolidated clay that occurs in the riverbed in some areas, especially in the lower reaches near Peterson Bridge. This material is resistant to erosion and underlies shallow areas in the stream. Where the resistant layer ends, an abrupt drop-off to deep water generally occurs. The fisherman can wade along the banks in some places where the stream is too deep at mid-channel, but some of the deep holes are right along the banks. The wading fisherman will have to take to the bank to get around some of the deep holes and runs. Overhanging brush, logjams, and steep cut banks in places can make such a maneuver extremely difficult. If you must go to the banks, try to climb out where the banks are low and well-protected by vegetation. Climbing the steep, sandy banks will cause erosion. The steeper banks on the Pine are generally on the outside of bends, with lower banks on the inside. There generally is a path of some sort along one or both banks of the Pine. These vary from well-marked trails to those indicated only by a faint trace of bent or broken vegetation.

Many bait and spin fishermen on the Pine do not wade at all, but find a spot where they can cast from the banks. Others restrict their wading to shallow areas near the banks. Obviously, the bait and spin fishermen do not need as much casting room as fly-fishermen.

The Pine River at the Dobson Bridge

On the Pine there are usually many more fishermen using bait or spinning lures than those using flies.

Because of the difficult wading, the fly-fisherman on the Pine may find it desirable to select a reach of river in which he can wade, become familiar with all the deep holes and other hazards, and concentrate his fishing in that area. Fishing the Pine is not like fishing the Holy Water on the Au Sable, where you can wade for miles down the river at mid-channel, fishing the good cover on both sides, easily avoiding the few deep holes and snags. If you try this on the Pine you will almost certainly come to grief.

The Pine has a large component of groundwater flow and consequently is a cold-water river with summer water temperatures usually below 70 degrees F. However, the Pine also has a large overland flow from the clay soils in the morainal hills of the watershed. After heavy rains the Pine rises rather quickly and becomes so cloudy that you cannot see the bottom even in the shallow areas. At such times wading, even along the banks, may be hazardous. Fly-fishing is nearly impossible, and the bait fisherman, fishing from the banks, has a better chance of success.

Another reason the Pine is not as popular with fly-fishermen as some of the other trout streams of the Lower Peninsula is that the insect hatches are relatively meager. Michigan fisheries biologists believe that the poor hatches on the Pine are due, at least in part, to the abrading action of the large bed load of sand that moves down the Pine.

The problem of the bed load of sand on the Pine was studied in detail by Edward A. Hansen (1971). He predicted that a complete streambed stabilization program would reduce the sediment load by about half and probably result in changes beneficial to trout. In 1990, local groups formed the Pine River Watershed Restoration Committee to work on controlling erosion on the Pine. Major sources of sand include road crossings within the watershed and stream bank erosion. Fishermen can help reduce stream bank erosion by entering and leaving the stream in places protected from erosion, as at canoe-landing ramps and along low banks with ample vegetative cover. Avoid climbing up or down the high sandy banks that are common along much of the Pine.

The Pine is a popular canoe trail, and there are several canoe liveries in the area. The Pine is not recommended for inexperienced boaters, but it can be floated by those of moderate competence at normal summer flows. Most of the wet canoers I encountered on the river said they had tipped over when the fast current swept them against overhanging branches, logjams, or other obstructions in the stream. At high flows, floating the Pine may be dangerous even for experienced boaters. Canoe liveries generally will not rent their boats when the river is high. A list of liveries currently in operation can be obtained from the U.S. Forest Service, 421 South Mitchell Street, Cadillac, MI 49601. The Forest Service requests that canoe-ists use the river from 9:00 A.M. to 6:00 P.M. only, leaving early morning and late evening hours for anglers. To avoid canoers, fisher-men are advised to fish before noon below Peterson Bridge or after 3:00 P.M. above Elm Flats.

The Pine is too fast and too narrow in most places above Peterson Bridge for easy fishing from a canoe. Overhanging brush, low sweepers, and recent blowdowns add to the difficulty. Some river guides now use flat-bottomed rowboats of the dory design (Mac-Kenzie River Boats) to fish the Pine. The oarsman guides and slows the boat by rowing as if headed upstream but allowing the boat to drift slowly downstream. This gives the fisherman more time to search and cover the favorable water.

The river flows in a complex system of meanders that make the river distance between two points more than double the overland distance. The U.S. Forest Service lists the river miles and approxi-mate time to float between some of the access points on the river as follows:

	Hours	Miles
Skookum Bridge to Walker Bridge	2	6.5
Walker Bridge to Lincoln Bridge	0.75	3
Lincoln Bridge to Elm Flats	1	3
Elm Flats to Dobson Bridge	2	6
Dobson Bridge to Peterson Bridge	2	6
Peterson Bridge to Low Bridge	2	6

The boat fisherman will, of course, have to allow additional time for his fishing. Probably the easiest way to boat fish the Pine is to float down to a likely spot shallow enough to wade safely, tie up or beach the canoe, and fish by wading. Be sure you do not trespass on private property.

The North and East Branches of the Pine come together about 3.5 miles west of the village of Tustin in Osceola County. From here the river flows generally southwest to the Lake County line, where it turns northwest, cutting across the northeastern part of Lake County and on into Wexford County. From Peterson Bridge it flows mainly westward into Manistee County, where it again turns northwest to enter the south arm of Tippy Pond in Manistee County.

A small, brush-lined stream in the headwaters, the Pine is about 40 feet wide and mostly 2 to 4 feet deep as it flows into Lake County. The riverbed is sand and gravel, with many cobbles and boulders. The flow is swift and the wading fisherman must watch out for boulders, deep holes, drowned logs, blowdowns, and sweepers.

As it flows across the northeast corner of Lake County the Pine is generally 40 to 70 feet wide and 2 to 4 feet deep, but with many deep holes that will overtop your waders and some that are over your head. The bottom is sand and gravel, cobbles, and boulders, with some hard clay. The sandy areas generally are in the deep holes and along the banks and in the slower water, as along the insides of some of the big bends. The riverbanks are alternately high and low, some more than 70 feet high. Numerous logs, boulders, and snags are a hazard to the wading fisherman, and the fast current can push him into deep holes that will go over his waders. Overhanging brush and blowdowns can also force the wading fisherman into deep water.

From the south line of Wexford County to Peterson Bridge the Pine is 40 to 80 feet wide, 2 to 5 feet deep, with some holes more than 6 feet deep. The bottom is mostly gravel, cobbles, boulders, and hard clay in the fast reaches and sand in the slower water. The hard clay forms ledges along the banks and fast, shallow riffles, overlain in places by boulders and cobbles. Parts of the stream here can be waded with care at low water if you avoid the deeper runs and fast water. There are few places where you can wade more than a few hundred feet without taking to the banks on one side or the other. The river cannot be safely waded at high flows.

Except at the public access sites, most of the river frontage above Walker Bridge is private land. Below Walker Bridge all the way to Peterson Bridge most of the land is public—a part of the Manistee National Forest, but there are numerous private riverfront holdings.

Accommodations

The city of Cadillac, northeast of the Pine, has many excellent motels and restaurants. Motels and restaurants also are available at

Reed City and Baldwin to the south. Fishing tackle and food are also available at the smaller villages of Tustin, Bristol, and Luther.

State forest campgrounds are on the river at Silver Creek and Lincoln Bridge. These are equipped with water supply, toilets, and picnic tables. Camping for four parties is also permitted at the access site below Edgetts Bridge and two access sites below Skookum Bridge.

The U.S. Forest Service has an excellent campground on the Pine at Peterson Bridge. The Forest Service also maintains canoe landings at Elm Flats, Dobson Bridge, and Peterson Bridge (north side), but camping is not permitted at these sites. Canoe liveries are available near Walker Bridge and Peterson Bridge.

Maps of the Pine

The stream channel and public roads leading to the access sites on the Pine are shown on the maps (figs. 89 and 90). The access sites on the maps are numbered in downstream order, starting with site 1, the Edgetts Bridge site northeast of Luther, and ending with site 8, at Peterson Bridge on M-37.

The road names in the Pine River area can be confusing. Some roads change names where they cross county lines. Many of the roads are identified by number. For example, in Wexford County, the east-west roads south of M-55 are numbered from north to south, No. 44½, No. 46, No. 48, No. 48½, No. 50, and No. 52. South of No. 52 Road, as you cross into Lake County, the numbering system changes. One mile south of No. 52 Road, the east-west road is 11 Mile Road, followed (going south) by 10 Mile, 9 Mile, 8 Mile, 7 Mile, 6 Mile, and 5 Mile Roads. Five Mile Road is 1½ miles north of the village of Luther. Adding to the confusion are the numbered roads of the U.S. Forest Service, which are totally unrelated to either of the county systems.

Site 1 (fig. 91) is a public access downstream from Edgetts Bridge on Raymond Road. Starting at the city of Cadillac, go south on U.S. 131 for 12 miles to Exit 168. Take this exit to the stop sign on 20 Mile Road. Turn right (west) on 20 Mile Road and go 5.4 miles to the village of Bristol. As you enter Lake County, 20 Mile Road becomes 8 Mile Road. The village of Bristol is at the intersection of 8 Mile Road and Raymond Road. Turn left (south) on Raymond Road and go 2.6 miles to a dirt road turning off to the right (west).

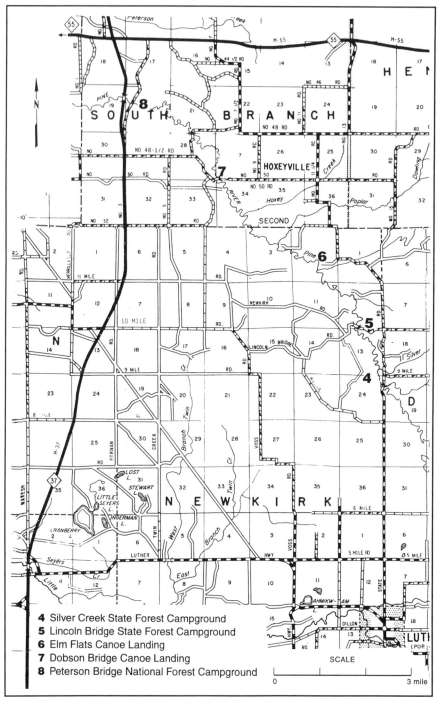

4 Silver Creek State Forest Campground
5 Lincoln Bridge State Forest Campground
6 Elm Flats Canoe Landing
7 Dobson Bridge Canoe Landing
8 Peterson Bridge National Forest Campground

SCALE

0   3 mile

Fig. 89. Location map of the Pine River, Silver Creek State Forest Campground to Peterson Bridge Campground

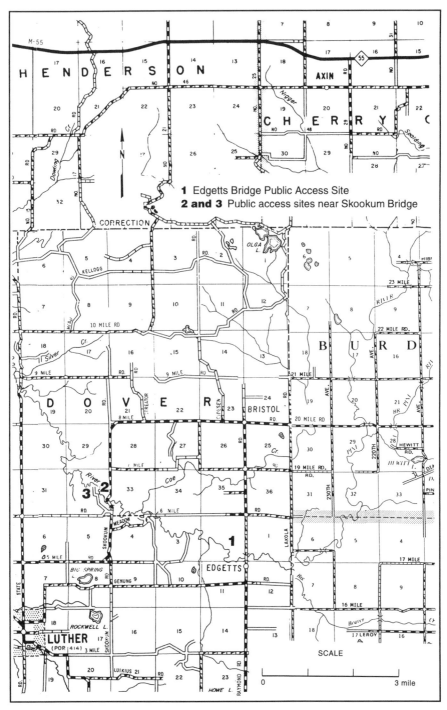

Fig. 90. Location map of the Pine River, Edgetts Bridge Public Access Site to public access sites near Skookum Bridge

This turnoff is just 0.25 mile (one-fourth mile) north of Edgetts Bridge. Turn right on this road and follow it 0.2 mile west to a fork in the road. Take the left fork and go another 0.2 mile to the access on high ground on the right bank of the Pine. A path leads from the parking area to a steep stairway down some 50 feet to the river.

The village of Luther is a convenient starting point for sites 2 through 6. To get to Luther from the south, take M-37 and U.S. 10 north out of Baldwin 3 miles to the point where U.S. 10 turns left (west) while M-37 continues on north. Continue north on M-37 for 8 miles to Luther Highway, a blacktop road leading off to the right (east). Follow Luther Highway east, south, and southeast 9 miles to the village of Luther.

To get to Luther from the north, starting at the intersection of M-37 and M-55, go south on M-37 about 12 miles to Luther Highway. Turn left (east) on Luther Highway and follow this road about 9 miles to the village of Luther.

To get to Luther from the village of Bristol, go south 3.5 miles on Raymond Road to the intersection with Genung Road 0.3 mile south of Edgetts Bridge. Turn right (west) on Genung Road and go 4.5 miles to a sharp left turn. Follow this turn to the south 0.8 mile, then right (west) 0.5 mile to the village of Luther.

Site 2 (fig. 92) is access on the right bank of the Pine downstream from Skookum Bridge. To get to site 2, go north out of Luther on State Road 1.5 miles to the intersection with 5 Mile Road. Turn right (east) on 5 Mile Road and go 2 miles to the intersection with Skookum Road. Turn left (north) on Skookum Road and go north 1.5 miles to a dirt road turning off to the left (west). You will cross the Pine on Skookum Bridge 0.2 mile before you get to the turnoff. Go west on this road 0.2 mile to the access site on the right bank of the Pine.

Or you can go west from Bristol on 8 Mile Road 3 miles to the intersection with Skookum Road. Turn left (south) on this road, following the blacktop, and go south 1.3 miles to a dirt road leading off to the right (west). (This road is 0.2 mile north of Skookum Bridge.) Turn right on this road and follow it 0.2 mile to the access site.

Site 3 (fig. 92) is a public access site on the left bank of the Pine downstream from site 2. To get to site 3, go north out of Luther on State Road 1.5 miles to 5 Mile Road. Turn right (east) on Five Mile Road and go 2 miles to the intersection with Skookum Road. Turn left (north) on Skookum Road and go 1 mile to the intersection with 6 Mile Road, a gravel road leading off to the left (west). Turn left on this road and go 0.25 mile (one-fourth of a mile) to a dirt road leading off to the right (north). Turn right on this road and go 0.8 mile north and northwest to the access site on the left bank. This site is about 0.2 mile northwest (downstream) from access site 2.

Site 4 (fig. 93) is Silver Creek State Forest Campground. Starting at the village of Luther, go north on State Road 5.4 miles to the campground on the left (west) side of the road. You will cross Walker Bridge 0.2 mile before you reach the campground.

Site 5 (fig. 94) is Lincoln Bridge State Forest Campground. Go 6.6 miles north of Luther (1.2 miles past Silver Creek Campground) on State Road, then turn left (west) on a gravel road (10 Mile Road) and go 0.4 mile to a dirt road leading off to the right (north) to the campground. If you continue another 0.2 mile west past this turnoff you will come to a canoe landing at the river's edge, but parking is not permitted here.

Site 6 (fig. 95) is Elm Flats Canoe Landing. Go north on State Road from Luther 7.6 miles (1 mile past the road to Lincoln Bridge Campground). The road turns northwest here for 0.7 mile, then west for 0.5 mile. Here the road turns right (north again), but you turn off to the left on a graded road that goes southwest then west 0.5 mile to Elm Flats Access Site on the right bank of the Pine. A stairway leads down from the parking lot to the canoe landing.

Site 7 (fig. 96) is Dobson Bridge Canoe Landing. Go south on M-37 from the junction with M-55 1.3 miles to Peterson Bridge. Continue south past the bridge 1.2 miles to the blacktop No. 48½ Road. Turn left (east) on this road and go 1.5 miles to where the blacktop turns north. You do not make this turn but continue on east and southeast 1 mile on a rough dirt and gravel road to Dobson Bridge. Cross the bridge and continue up the hill about 0.1 mile to the parking area on the left (north) side of the road. A stairway leads down from the parking area to the canoe landing on the river.

Site 8 (fig. 97) is the U.S. Forest Service Campground at Peterson Bridge. Go south on M-37 from the junction with M-55 1.3 miles to Peterson Bridge. Continue south past the bridge another 0.2 mile to the turn off on the left (east) to the campground. There is a parking area on the left just before you get to the camping area. A canoe landing is on the other (north) side of the river, and a large parking area is available there.

Site No. 1. Edgetts Bridge Public Access Site

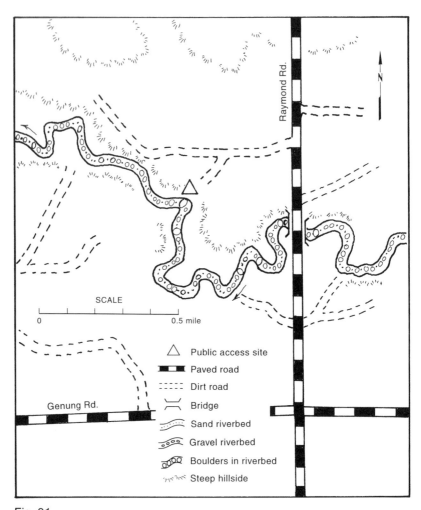

SCALE

0   0.5 mile

△   Public access site

▮▯▮   Paved road

-----   Dirt road

⏑   Bridge

Sand riverbed

Gravel riverbed

Boulders in riverbed

Steep hillside

Raymond Rd.

Genung Rd.

N

Fig. 91

Camping for four parties is permitted here. An outdoor toilet is provided but there is no water supply. The Pine is 20 to 40 feet wide here, and 2 to 4 feet deep, with deeper runs and holes. A hole that will overtop your waders is near the entrance point at the base of the steps. The bottom is mostly gravel, cobbles, and boulders, with some sand and clay. The flow is fast to very fast, and wading is difficult, even at low flows. At high flows, wading is impossible. The banks are alternately high and low, with a very high right bank at the entrance point. The banks are lined with much brush. The abundant trout cover includes overhanging brush, drowned logs, boulders, and deep holes. These same features that make good cover for trout are a hazard to the wading fisherman. The very high bank here makes this a poor place to launch a canoe.

Site Nos. 2 and 3. Public Access
Sites near Skookum Bridge

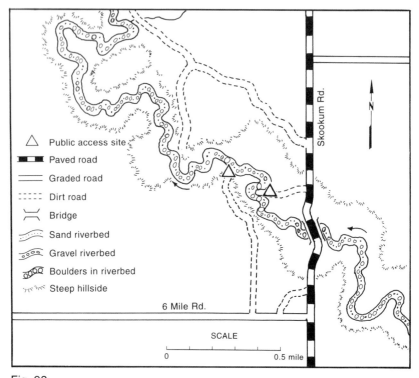

Fig. 92

Camping is also permitted at these sites, limited to four camping parties. The sites are furnished with privies and picnic tables. The river is 40 to 60 feet wide and mostly less than 4 feet deep with some deeper runs and holes. Bottom is mostly gravel, cobbles, and boulders in the fast runs and sand in the slower waters. Banks are low and mucky in places and high and sandy in others. Some banks at the outsides of bends are more than 50 feet high. Banks are lined with brush, hardwood, and some conifer. The stream velocity is moderate to fast at low flows, fast at high water. Parts of the river can be waded with care at normal low flows, but unwadable at high. Boulders, soft sand, drowned logs, snags, fast water, and deep holes are hazards to the wading fisherman at all times. Site No. 3 on the left bank is a convenient spot for launching canoes.

Site No. 4. Silver Creek State Forest Campground

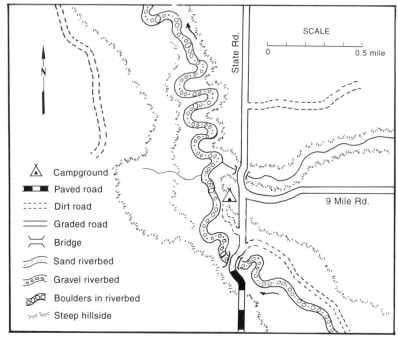

Campground

Paved road

Dirt road

Graded road

Bridge

Sand riverbed

Gravel riverbed

Boulders in riverbed

Steep hillside

State Rd.

SCALE

0   0.5 mile

9 Mile Rd.

Fig. 93

This campground is furnished with water supply (hand pumps), picnic tables, and toilets. The river is 40 to 60 feet wide and 2 to 4 feet deep at midstream with deeper holes. Bottom is gravel and boulders in the fast water and sand in places along the banks and in slower runs. The banks are low in places but mostly high and sandy, more than 50 feet in some places. Bank cover is brush and hardwood with some conifer. Trout cover is abundant. Stream velocity is fast at all times and very fast at high water. The river can be waded at normal low flows, watching out for boulders, snags, deep holes, and soft sand in places as at the mouth of Silver Creek. You will have to take to the banks to get around some of the deep areas. Again, be careful that you do not cause erosion of the banks. At high flows, it is not safe to try to wade here.

Site No. 5. Lincoln Bridge State Forest Campground

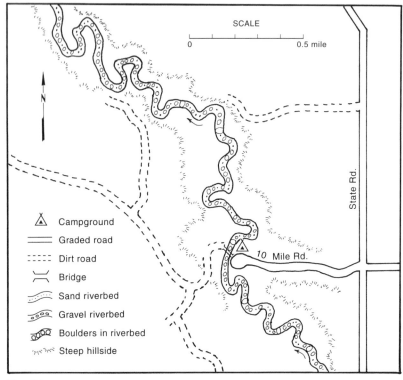

SCALE

0   0.5 mile

State Rd.

△ Campground
── Graded road
┅┅ Dirt road
⊢⊣ Bridge
≈≈ Sand riverbed
∘∘∘ Gravel riverbed
○○○ Boulders in riverbed
ᵛᵛᵛ Steep hillside

△ 10 Mile Rd.

Fig. 94

This campground is well supplied with hand pumps, picnic tables, and toilets. The camping and parking areas are on high ground above the canoe landing. Cars are not permitted in the camping areas. The landing area is restricted to launching and pickup of canoes, and parking is not permitted here. Lincoln Bridge, just downstream from the landing ramp, is a narrow bridge not for ordinary passenger cars or trucks. The Pine here is 40 to 60 feet wide and 2 to 4 feet deep with some deeper runs and holes. Bottom is mostly gravel, cobbles, and boulders in the fast reaches and sand in the slower areas. Banks are alternately high and low, but mostly high. Bank vegetation is predominantly brush and conifer, with hardwood in the uplands. The flow is fast at normal flows and very fast at high water. The river can be waded in places, but some parts are too fast and deep even at low flows. At high flows the river cannot be safely waded. Boulders, snags, and a fast current make wading difficult at all times.

Site No. 6. Elm Flats Canoe Landing

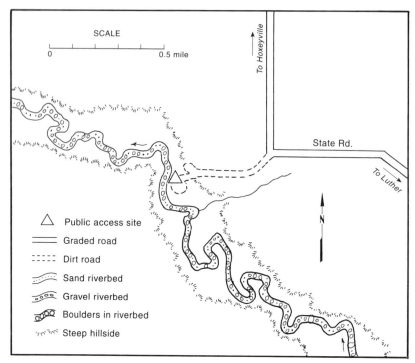

Fig. 95

There is a hand pump and toilets at this canoe access, but camping is not permitted here. The parking area is on high ground above the launching ramp. A stairway leads down from the parking area to the ramp, a convenient spot to enter the river. The Pine is 40 to 80 feet wide here and 2 to 4 feet deep with deeper holes. The riverbed is mostly gravel in the fast water, sand in the slower areas. The river banks are generally low, 3 to 5 feet, with some higher banks at the outsides of bends. Bank vegetation is mostly hardwood and brush with some cedar. There is some bottom vegetation here. Stream velocity is moderate at low flows, fast at high. The river can be waded with care at normal low flows, avoiding the deep holes, snags, boulders, and soft sand. At high flows the river cannot be safely waded. The Pine is wide and open enough here for fly-fishing.

Site No. 7. Dobson Bridge Canoe Landing

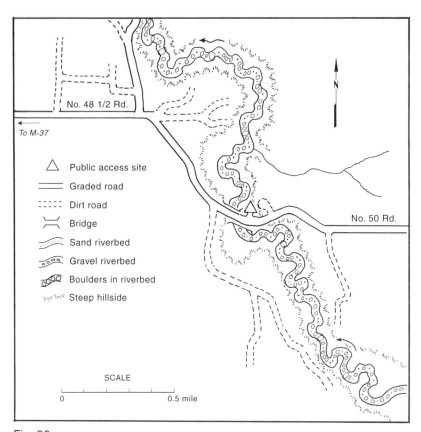

N

No. 48 1/2 Rd.

To M-37

No. 50 Rd.

△ Public access site

━━━ Graded road

┄┄┄ Dirt road

Bridge

Sand riverbed

Gravel riverbed

Boulders in riverbed

Steep hillside

SCALE

0   0.5 mile

Fig. 96

Like Elm Flats, this canoe access is equipped with a hand pump and toilet, but camping is not permitted. The parking area is on high ground above the launching area. The river is 40 to 70 feet wide and 3 to 4 feet deep with deeper holes. Bottom is mostly gravel, cobbles, and boulders, with sand in the slower areas. Banks are alternately high and low, with brush, cedar, and hardwood cover. There are some streamside cabins in this area. The velocity is moderate at low flows in the wider areas, fast in the narrow chutes. There is fair wading at normal low flows downstream from the bridge if you avoid the deep holes and narrow chutes. Do not try to wade under the bridge. The river is unwadable at high flows.

Site No. 8. Peterson Bridge National Forest Campground

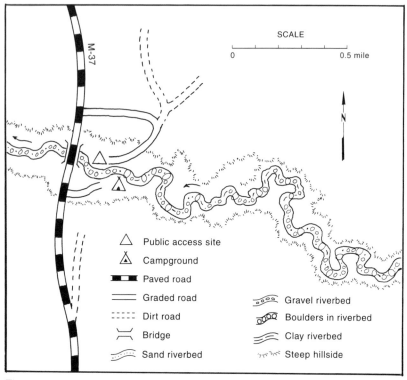

SCALE

0   0.5 mile

M-37

N

△ Public access site

▲ Campground

▆▆▆ Paved road

─── Graded road

----- Dirt road

⋈ Bridge

〰️ Sand riverbed

〰️ Gravel riverbed

〰️ Boulders in riverbed

〰️ Clay riverbed

Steep hillside

Fig. 97

The campground is on the left (south) bank of the river above the bridge. The campground is well equipped with water, toilets, and picnic tables. Camping is at numbered sites and the fee is $4.00 per night per camping party. On the other side of the river is a canoe landing and picnic area with ample parking. This is a busy area on weekends but not too crowded on weekdays. If you are not camping you can park in the picnic area and walk down to the river at the launching site.

The Pine is 50 to 75 feet wide here and 2 to 5 feet deep with holes and runs that are over your head. Bottom materials are gravel, boulders, and hard clay in the fast areas, sand in the slow. Where the bottom material is hard clay one step can take you from ankle-deep water to a hole over your head. Velocity is fast at low water and very fast at high. There is some wadable water at low normal flows at the canoe landing and a short distance downstream toward the bridge. Upstream from the canoe landing are a series of boulder riffles and hard clay with some sand in the intervening areas. Wading in the boulder riffles is difficult to impossible. The hard clay resembling bedrock restricts the river in places to a narrow channel of very fast water that should not be attempted by the wading fisherman.

The stream banks above the landing are mostly high to very high, some more than 50 feet high. Some of the paths along the river are along the top of high-cut sand banks. The paths run very close to the edge in places and may be undercut. The unwary fisherman could take a fall here. Forest cover is mostly hardwood with some conifer. The banks are not as brushy as in some upstream reaches.

Jordan River

Native brook trout inhabited the Jordan long before any trout were planted in Michigan streams. The Jordan was the source of the first brook trout planted in the Au Sable River system. The Jordan remains a good brook trout fishery in the upper reaches and has a good population of browns in the lower river. The resident rainbows are mostly small fish, less than 10 inches, that have not yet made their way back to Lake Charlevoix and Lake Michigan. The lower river provides a good fishery of steelhead and lake-run browns. The *Hexagenia* hatch begins later on the Jordan than on most Michigan streams, probably because the Jordan has relatively cold summer water temperatures. The hatch of these big mayflies usually begins in early July in the lower river and travels upstream to reach Pinney Bridge in early August.

From the headwaters in the morainal hills west of Elmira the Jordan flows generally to the southwest in wide looping meanders to near the Jordan River National Hatchery, where it turns westward in a relatively straight but braided channel past Pinney Bridge. This part of the river is entirely in public lands, a part of the Mackinac State Forest. Jordan River Road generally parallels the meanders of the river above the hatchery and crosses the stream in several places.

There are several places above the hatchery where you can pull off the road and fish this part of the Jordan. The river here is about 15 to 30 feet wide and mostly 1 to 3 feet deep, with some deeper holes. Bottom is mostly sand with some fine gravel. Wading is relatively easy. Most of the trout caught in this part of the river are small.

Below the fish hatchery to Pinney Bridge the Jordan flows generally westward in a relatively straight channel to Pinney Bridge. Pinney Bridge Road parallels the river on the south. The river is braided here with individual channels from 10 to 30 feet wide and 1 to 4 feet deep with some deeper holes. Bottom is mostly sand, with small patches of fine gravel and many drowned logs. Wading is difficult in places because of fast current and deep holes, but mainly because of the many drowned logs that crisscross the stream. It is easy to get your foot jammed between logs. The Old Bridge access is in this part of the river, and there is a good access at Pinney Bridge.

Below Pinney Bridge the Jordan flows northwestward in braided channels to near the junction with Green River. Here it turns north and flows more rapidly in a single channel 30 to 50 feet wide and 2 to 4 feet deep with some deeper runs and holes. The riverbed becomes less sandy downstream, and at Graves Crossing the bottom is mostly gravel, cobbles, and boulders in the faster reaches and sand in the slower areas. The flow becomes faster here as the river drops 5 meters (16.4 feet) in 0.9 of a mile, or about 18 feet per mile.

Hard white clay or marl, overlain in places by gravel, cobbles, or boulders, begins to appear in the riverbed below Graves Crossing. The white clay is resistant to erosion and forms ledges in places that resemble limestone bedrock. This material appears intermittently in

The Jordan River below Webster Bridge

the streambed at least as far downstream as Chestonia Bridge. The fast current and deep runs make wading difficult at all times and impossible at high water. Below Chestonia Bridge the Jordan becomes sandier again as the stream gradient decreases to about 10 feet per mile. As it nears the site of an abandoned railroad crossing, the Jordan flows relatively slowly in a deep, wide channel with sand bottom that somewhat resembles the "Stillwater" on the Au Sable.

Below the old railroad crossing the Jordan narrows again, velocity increases, and there is more gravel on the bottom along with a scattering of boulders. The river becomes sandier again downstream, and from Webster Bridge downstream the Jordan is mostly sand bottom, 50 to 75 feet wide and 2 to 4 feet deep with some runs and holes more than 5 feet deep.

Below Rogers Road Bridge the Jordan deepens and widens as it approaches the south arm of Lake Charlevoix.

About 90 percent of the flow of the Jordan comes from groundwater, making it one of the coldest, most stable, and clearest streams in Michigan's Lower Peninsula. Nevertheless, the flow of the river does increase after heavy rains, especially in the early spring. In places where wading is marginal at normal flows, an increase of even a few inches can make wading difficult to impossible.

From the headwaters to near Graves Crossing the Jordan is too narrow and choked with logjams and brush to make canoeing comfortable. From Graves Crossing to Lake Charlevoix the Jordan can be floated by boaters of moderate competence, but it is not well suited to boat fishing except for the last leg below Rogers Road Bridge. It is too narrow for easy fly casting from a boat and too fast for effective fishing of any kind. Those who like to use a boat to reach otherwise inaccessible reaches of the river can float down to a likely area not too deep for wading, tie up or beach the boat, and fish by wading. The Jordan below Graves Crossing does not have the complex system of meanders found on the Pine or Pere Marquette. The downstream distance, following the meanders of the stream, is only about 25 percent greater than the overland distance between any two points on the river.

Accommodations

The town of East Jordan at the mouth of the river probably is the most convenient headquarters for fishing the Jordan. Good food, lodging, and fishing tackle are available here. The town of Gaylord, east of the upper river, and the town of Mancelona, to the south, also have good restaurants, motels, and fishing tackle. Camping is permitted at the municipal park at East Jordan, and the Forest Campground at Graves Crossing is equipped with water supply, toilets, and picnic tables. A walk-in campground located north of Pinney Bridge is equipped with water supply and toilets. Spaces usually are available at any of these campgrounds. Camping is also permitted on state forest lands except where specifically prohibited or where a developed campground is available within one mile. Prospective campers in undeveloped sites should obtain a Camp Registration Card from any Department of Natural Resources field office. A canoe livery east of the bridge at Graves Crossing is available for floating the Jordan.

Maps of the Jordan

The location map (fig. 98) shows the stream channel and public roads leading to the access sites on the Jordan. The city of East Jordan is a convenient starting point for the access sites on the river. Site 1 (fig. 99) is about 11 miles southeast of East Jordan and about 1 mile southwest of the Jordan River National Fish Hatchery. To get to site 1, go west out of East Jordan 1 mile on Ellsworth Road (crossing the bridge over the south arm of Lake Charlevoix) to the intersection with M-66. Turn left (south) on M-66 and go southeast 11.3 miles to Pinney Bridge Road. Turn left (east) on this gravel road and go 4.2 miles to site 1 on the left (north) side of the road. There is a small parking area here and a wooden stairway leading down to the river.

Site 2 (fig. 100) is at Pinney Bridge about 2.5 miles west of site 1. Starting at the intersection of M-66 and Pinney Bridge Road, go east on Pinney Bridge Road 1.7 miles to the turnoff to Pinney Bridge on the left (north) side of the road. Pinney Bridge is blocked to auto traffic now, but there is a parking area here next to the bridge and you can walk across the bridge and on up to the camping area on high ground northeast of the bridge.

Site 3 (fig. 101) is at Graves Crossing State Forest Campground. Go west from East Jordan 1 mile on Ellsworth Road to the intersection with M-66. Turn left (south) on M-66 and go 9.5 miles southeast to a gravel road turning off to the left (east). Turn left

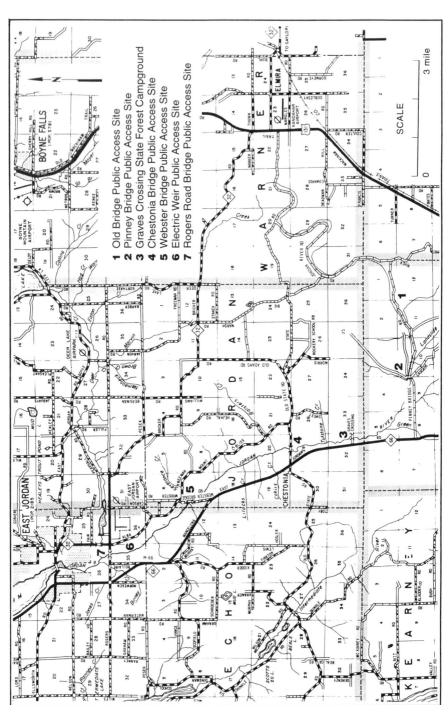

1 Old Bridge Public Access Site
2 Pinney Bridge Public Access Site
3 Graves Crossing State Forest Campground
4 Chestonia Bridge Public Access Site
5 Webster Bridge Public Access Site
6 Electric Weir Public Access Site
7 Rogers Road Bridge Public Access Site

Fig. 98. Location map of the Jordan River, headwaters to East Jordan

on this road and go 0.1 mile to a dirt road on the left leading northeast to the campground on the west side of the river.

Site 4 (fig. 102) is Chestonia Bridge. Again, go west from East Jordan 1 mile on Ellsworth Road to M-66. Turn left (south) on M-66 and go 7.7 miles to Old State Road. Turn left (east) here and go 0.4 mile to the bridge. There is limited parking here on the south side of the road, both east and west of the bridge. Two cars can park off the road, one behind the other, on the south side of the road west of the bridge. Off-road parking on the north side of the road east of the bridge has now been blocked by wood posts.

Site 5 (fig. 103) is just below Webster Bridge. Go west from East Jordan 1 mile on Ellsworth Road, then turn south on M-66 and go southeast 5.3 miles to Webster Bridge Road, a gravel road on the left leading north. Turn a sharp left on this road and go north 0.7 mile, crossing Webster Bridge and on to the parking area on the left side of the road just downstream from the bridge.

Site 6 (fig. 104) is on the right (east) bank of the Jordan 2 miles south of East Jordan. Go south from East Jordan 1.5 miles on M-32. Then, where M-32 turns left (east) continue on south 0.5 mile on Mt. Bliss Road (Alba Road on the county highway map) to a gravel road turning off to the right (west). Turn right on this road and go west 0.3 mile to the parking area on the right bank of the Jordan.

Site 7 (fig. 105) is off Rogers Road about 1.5 miles upstream from the mouth of the Jordan. Go south from East Jordan 1.5 miles on M-32 to Rogers Road. Turn right (west) on this road and go 0.2 mile to the parking area on the right (north) side of the road east of the bridge.

Site No. 1. Old Bridge Public Access Site

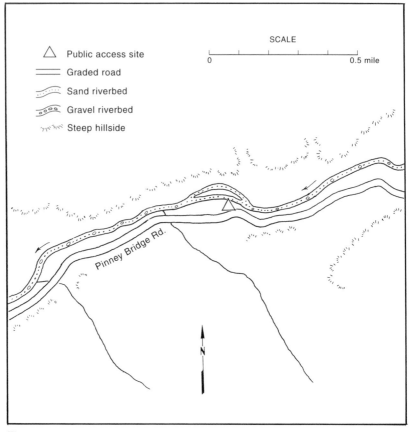

Fig. 99

The Jordan is a shallow, sandy stream here, mostly 1 to 2 feet deep with some deeper holes. Few of the holes would overtop your waders. The stream is much braided with individual channels as narrow as 2 feet and as wide as 30 feet. Total width is about 30 to 40 feet. The stream divides into two main channels about 100 yards above the old bridge, forming a sort of low island about 200 yards long. The stream-bed is mostly sand with some muck and patches of fine gravel. The velocity is moderate in the wider channels but can be fast in some of the narrower ones. Banks are mostly low, lined with cedar, brush, and some hardwood. The chief obstacles to the wading fisherman are drowned logs and snags, soft sand, deeper holes, and fast flow in some of the channels. The drowned logs and deep holes provide very good trout cover. The stream is wide and open enough for fly-fishing.

Site No. 2. Pinney Bridge Public Access Site

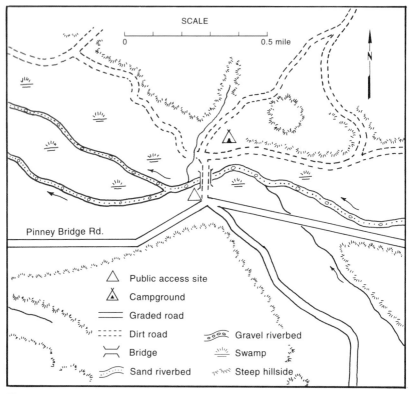

SCALE

0   0.5 mile

N

Pinney Bridge Rd.

△ Public access site
Ⓐ Campground
═ Graded road
┅ Dirt road   ∘∘∘ Gravel riverbed
⊃⊂ Bridge   Swamp
∿ Sand riverbed   Steep hillside

Fig. 100

There is a foot trail across the bridge to a campsite on high ground about 400 yards northeast of the bridge. The campsite is equipped with a hand pump and toilet. Landslide Creek joins the Jordan above Pinney Bridge, and the stream is wider and deeper and flows faster than at the Old Bridge site. The braided channels here total 40 to 80 feet, and individual channels are 2 to 4 feet deep, with many deeper holes. The bottom is mostly sand with small patches of gravel and some muck. Small patches of dark, almost black, bottom vegetation are in some of the channels. The stream channels in many places are choked with a crisscross of drowned logs, like giant jackstraws. Trout cover, including drowned logs and deep holes, is most abundant. Banks are low and swampy, 1 to 3 feet, lined with cedar, spruce, hemlock, brush, and some hardwood. The jumble of drowned logs makes wading extremely difficult in some places and dangerous to impossible in others. Other hazards to the wading fisherman are deep holes, fast flow in some channels, and soft sand. This is not the kind of water you would want to wade in alone at night.

Site No. 3. Graves Crossing State Forest Campground

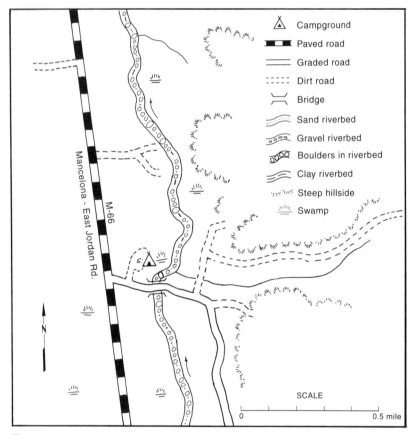

Fig. 101

The campground is equipped with water supply, toilets, and picnic tables. This is the starting point for most canoe travel on the Jordan. Green River joins the Jordan about a half-mile upstream, and the stream flows fast and deep in a single channel. The river is 30 to 50 feet wide and 2 to 4 feet deep with deeper holes. The bottom is gravel, cobbles, and boulders, with some sand and muck. Patches of hard white clay or marl are exposed in the streambed below the bridge. Banks are low, 1 to 3 feet, forested with spruce, popple, cedar, and pine, with some brushy areas. The velocity is fast to very fast. The fast current and deep holes, over your waders in places, make wading very difficult here. Drowned logs, boulders, and some soft sand and muck are additional hazards. Trout cover is very good. The river is wide and open enough for fly-fishing.

Site No. 4. Chestonia Bridge Public Access Site

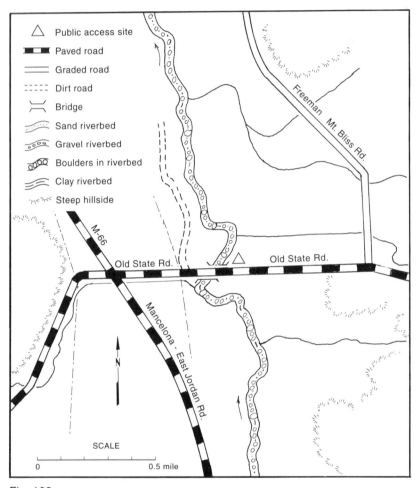

Legend:
- △ Public access site
- Paved road
- Graded road
- Dirt road
- Bridge
- Sand riverbed
- Gravel riverbed
- Boulders in riverbed
- Clay riverbed
- Steep hillside

Freeman Mt. Bliss Rd.

M-66

Old State Rd.

Old State Rd.

Mancelona - East Jordan Rd.

N

SCALE

0   0.5 mile

Fig. 102

The river is 40 to 80 feet wide and 2 to 4 feet deep with some holes over your waders. Bottom is gravel, cobbles, and boulders, with sand in the slower areas. Patches of hard white clay or marl are exposed in the streambed above and below the bridge, in places forming ledges that resemble limestone bedrock. Banks are mostly low, but some-what higher than at Graves Crossing. Bank vegetation is cedar, spruce, popple, and brush. Wading here is somewhat easier than at Graves Crossing if you watch out for deep holes and ledges of hard clay. One such ledge, about 180 yards upstream from the bridge, extends across most of the channel. If you are wading facing the rising sun you can trip over this ledge. Trout cover is good and there is ample room for fly casting.

Site No. 5. Webster Bridge Public Access Site

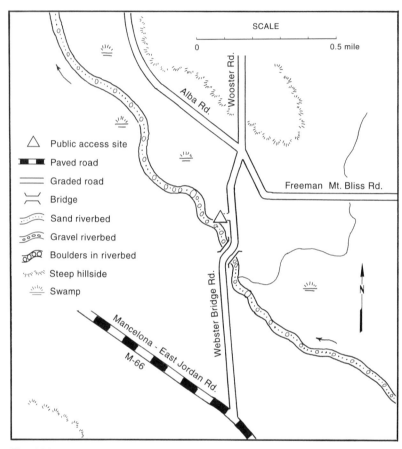

Fig. 103

There is a toilet at this parking lot but no other facilities. A United States Geological Survey gaging station is at the site. The river varies in width from 40 to 65 feet and is mostly 3 to 4 feet deep with holes over your waders. Bottom is sand and gravel, with more sand than in the upstream reaches. Banks are low, lined with cedar, brush, and some hardwood. There are some grassy areas by riverside homes. Parts of the river can be waded with caution, but the private river frontage makes it difficult to get around some of the deep runs. Drowned logs, snags, brush, and boulders add to the difficulty. Watch out for broken concrete under the bridge and for a short distance upstream. Trout cover is very good. The river is wide and open enough for fly-fishing. This is a popular canoe landing and take-out point.

Site No. 6. Electric Weir Public Access Site

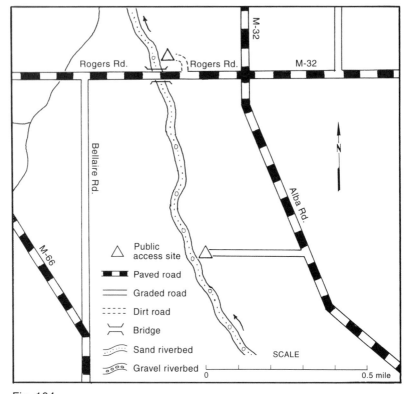

Fig. 104

There is a parking area and portable toilet, possibly temporary, here. Wooden landing docks above and below the electric weir are provided for boaters to portage around the weir. Do not attempt to float across the high-voltage weir. The river is 50 to 60 feet wide and 3 to 5 feet deep, with deeper holes. Bottom is sand with very little gravel. The gravel at the site has been hauled in. Banks are low, 2 to 5 feet, lined with hardwood and cedar and some brush. The flow is fast and wading is very difficult to impossible. There is a path down the right (east) bank that is used by fishermen, but the river frontage is mostly private.

Site No. 7. Rogers Road Bridge
Public Access Site

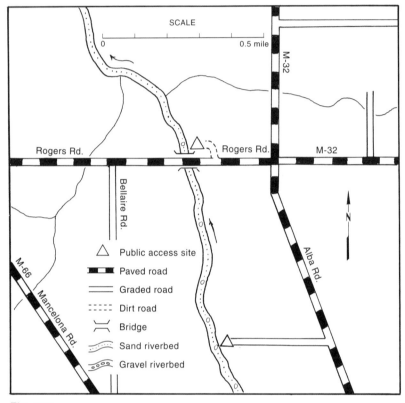

Fig. 105

There is a parking area and toilet here but no other facilities. Riverside houses and well-kept lawns are on both sides of the river, and all frontage except for the access site is private land. The river is 50 to 75 feet wide and 2 to 4 feet deep with some deeper holes. Bottom is mostly sand. The small area of gravel at the access point probably has been hauled in. The flow is moderate in the wide areas and fast where the river narrows. Wading downstream a few hundred yards from the access point is fairly easy at normal summer flows, but there are some deep holes that will overtop your waders, and you cannot take to the banks without trespassing on private property. Wading upstream from the bridge against the current is difficult and soon becomes impossible where the stream is narrow, fast, and deep. Trout cover is good except by the houses, where it is sparse.

References Cited

Alexander, Gaylord R. *Results of Fishing and Angler Questionnaire on the South Branch of the Au Sable, Mason Tract, Crawford County, Michigan, during the Burrowing Mayfly Hatch, 1973.* Fisheries Research Report No. 1808. Lansing: Michigan Department of Natural Resources, 1974.

Alexander, Gaylord, R., and Hanson, Edward A. "Sand Sediments in a Michigan Trout Stream, Pt 2. Effects of Reducing Sand Bedload on a Trout Population." *North American Journal of Fisheries Management* 3 (1982): 365–72.

———. *Effects of Sand Bedload Sediment on a Brook Trout Population.* Fisheries Research Report No. 1906. Lansing: Michigan Department of Natural Resources, 1983.

Charles, Gordon. "Those Good Old Fishing Days." In *Currents of the Boardman,* 82–88. Traverse City: Grand Traverse County Historical Society, 1982.

Dennis, Jerry, and Date, Craig. *Canoeing Michigan Rivers.* Davison, MI: Friede Publications, 1986.

Fenske, Janice L. Survey Report on the Upper Black River System. Draft manuscript. Hunt Creek Research Station, Lewiston, MI: 1992.

Gowing, Howard, and Alexander, Gaylord R. *Population Dynamics of Trout in Some Streams of the Northern Lower Peninsula of Michigan.* Fisheries Research Report No. 1877. Lansing: Michigan Department of Natural Resources, 1980.

Hanson, Edward A. *Sediment in a Michigan Trout Stream, Its Source, Movement, and Some Effects on Fish Habitat.* Research Paper NC-59. St. Paul: North Central Forest Experiment Station, U.S. Forest Service, 1971.

Ingle, Don. "A Century of the Outdoors around Baldwin." *Lake County Star,* July 27, 1973.

Inglis, James Gale. *Northern Michigan Handbook for Travelers.* Petoskey: George E. Sprang, 1898. Reprint. Grand Rapids: Black Letter Press, 1974.

Jenson, Margaret. *The South Branch of the Au Sable as Seen by Margaret Jenson.* N.p., 1982.

Leonard, Justin W., and Leonard, Fannie A. *Noteworthy Records of Caddis Flies from Michigan, with Descriptions of New Species.* Occasional Papers No. 520. Ann Arbor: University of Michigan Museum of Zoology, 1949.

———. *Mayflies of Michigan Trout Streams.* Bloomfield Hills: Cranbrook Institute of Science, 1962.

Melkild, Martin. "Where Indian Trails and Rivers Meet." In *Currents of the Boardman*, 12–16. Traverse City: Grand Traverse County Historical Society, 1982.

Merna, James W., and Alexander, Gaylord R. *Effects of Snowmelt Runoff on pH and Alkalinity of Trout Streams in Northern Michigan*. Fisheries Technical Report No. 83-2. Lansing: Michigan Department of Natural Resources, 1983.

Merron, Glenn S. *Growth Rate of Brown Trout* (Salmo trutta) *in Areas of the Au Sable River, Michigan, before and after Domestic Sewage Diversion*. Fisheries Research Report No. 1900. Lansing: Michigan Department of Natural Resources, 1982.

Mershon, William B. *Recollections of My Fifty Years of Hunting and Fishing*. Boston: Stratford Co., 1923.

Norris, Thadeus. "The Michigan Grayling." *Scribner's Magazine*, 19, no. 2 (1879).

Peterson, Kenneth L. "Match the Michigan Hatches." *Michigan Sportsman*, May/June, 1983, pp. 44–47, 76–78.

Rayle, S. Louise. "It All Began on the Boardman." In *Currents of the Boardman*, 89–104. Traverse City: Grand Traverse County Historical Society, 1982.

Swan, Steve. "Sturgeon River Improvement Proposal." *Michigan Trout*. January/February, 1984.

Vandemark, Jerry. *A History of the Rifle River Area*. Michigan Department of Natural Resources, 1975.

Other Sources of Information

Trout Streams of Michigan, volumes 1 and 2, published by the Michigan United Conservation Clubs, gives a wealth of information on more than forty-six trout streams in both the Upper and Lower peninsulas of Michigan. Available from the Michigan United Conservation Clubs, P.O. Box 30235, Lansing, Michigan 48909. Michigan United Conservation Clubs also publishes a book of Michigan county maps. These maps show rivers, roads, and state lands, and are most useful to the angler.

A series of *Trout Angler's Guides* to Michigan trout streams has been published by the Paul H. Young Chapter of Trout Unlimited, Clarkston, Michigan. Maps showing the channel width and depth and character of bed and banks are included with the guides.

A series of *Hydrologic Atlases* showing the flow characteristics, water quality, and channel, bed, and banks have been published by the U.S. Geological Survey. Atlases of the Pigeon (Ha-333), the Black (HA-354), the Sturgeon (HA-353), the Pere Marquette (HA-384), the Rifle (HA-426), the Manistee (HA-436) and the Au Sable (HA-527) are available from the U.S. Geological Survey, Reston, Virginia 22092.

U.S. Geological Survey topographic maps accurately show the drainage pattern and topography of most areas of Michigan. They also show many roads not shown on the county highway maps. These are generally the best maps to carry to avoid getting lost when fishing wilderness areas. As of 1993 the entire state has been mapped at a scale of 1:24,000 or 1:25,000 (2.5 inches = about 1 mile). Some quadrangles of particular interest to trout fishermen on the streams described in this book are listed here.

Sturgeon, Pigeon, and Black Rivers: Burt Lake, Indian River, Legrand, Wildwood, Wolverine, Afton, Tower, Onaway, Vanderbilt, Green Timbers, Hardwood Lake, Silver Lake, Lake Geneva, Gaylord, Sparr, Saunders Creek, Hetherton, and Atlanta 7.5-minute quadrangles.

Pere Marquette River: Custer, Tallman, Townsend Lake, Baldwin, Big Star Lake, and Marlborough 7.5-minute quadrangles.

Manistee River: Frederic, Black Creek, Lake Margrethe, Sharon, Fletcher, and Cote Dame Marie 7.5-minute quadrangles.

Boardman River: Mayfield, Jacks Landing, Kingsley, and Walton 7.5-minute quadrangles.

Au Sable River: Grayling, Wakeley, and Luzerne NW 7.5-minute quadrangles.

South Branch Au Sable: Roscommon North, Eldorado, and Luzerne NW 7.5-minute quadrangles.

North Branch Au Sable: Lovells and Luzerne NW 7.5-minute quadrangles.

Rifle River: Rose City and Selkirk 7.5-minute quadrangles.

Quadrangle maps may be ordered from the Michigan Department of Natural Resources, Geological Survey Division, P.O. Box 30256, Lansing, MI 48909. Quadrangle maps may also be ordered from Michigan United Conservation Clubs, P.O. Box 30235, Lansing, MI 48909.

Index

Acid rain, 16–17
Adams, C. F., 12
Adams (fly), 12
Aesthetic quality of streams, 1, 17, 94, 120
Agriculture, 2, 210
Alba Road, 275
Antrim County, 95
Aquatic vegetation, 17
Au Sable River, 4, 7, 17, 20, 24–51, 52, 76, 94, 95, 120
Au Sable riverboat, 27
Au Sable River Canoe State Forest Campground, 29, 32–33
Au Sable State Forest, 217, 221

Babbit, Rube, 26
Bait fishing, 2, 35, 63, 83, 85, 103, 113, 127, 142, 151, 165, 179, 199
Baldwin, 225, 227, 228, 230
Banks. See Riverbanks
Barber Bridge, 177
Bed. See Riverbed
Bed load (sand), 248
Beds, spawning, 15, 19, 26, 94, 172, 194
Black River, 3, 96, 142, 170–91
Black River Ranch, 171, 185
Black River Road, 177
Blue Lake Road, 176
Blue Lakes Club, 185
Boardman, Captain Harry, 194
Boardman River, 3, 12, 192–207
Boat fishing, 8, 26, 49, 54, 96, 120, 144, 171, 193, 225
Boating safety, 8–9

BOD (biochemical oxygen demand), 17
Bottom materials, 5, 6
Bower, Seymour, 3
Bowman Bridge, 224, 228, 229, 236, 238
Bowman Bridge Public Access Site, 228, 229, 230, 238–39
Boyne River, 4
Bristol (village), 251, 254
Brook trout, 3–5, 78, 170, 172, 227
Brown Bridge Dam, 193
Brown Bridge Pond, 192, 193, 207
Brown Bridge Road, 195, 197, 200, 202, 204, 205, 206, 207
Brown Bridge Road Public Access Site, 196, 197, 204–5
Brown trout, 3–5, 43, 52, 75, 93, 103, 105, 118, 131, 142, 192, 201, 205, 208, 224
Burt Lake, 142
Burt Lake State Park, 145
Burton's Landing, 24, 30, 35
Burton's Landing Road, 30, 34
Burton's Landing State Forest Campground, 28, 34–35

"Caddis" hatch, 24, 33, 47
Cadillac (city), 246, 250, 251
Cameron Bridge, 95, 96, 100, 104–5
Camping, 7
Camp Registration Cards, 8
Canoe Harbor Road, 56, 59
Canoe Harbor State Forest Campground, 56, 59, 72–73
Canoe liveries, 27, 54, 97, 227

Canoe safety, 8–9, 144, 172, 225
Carrs Road, 230, 236
Carscallen's Canoe Rental, 223
Castle Public Access Site, The, 53, 58, 66–67
CCC Bridge, 96, 100
CCC Bridge State Forest Campground, 96, 97, 112–13
Chase (village), 224
Chase Bridge, 53, 54, 56, 58, 59, 60
Chase Bridge Public Access Site, 58, 62–63
Chase Bridge Road, 57, 58, 59, 62
Cheboygan County, 124
Chestonia Bridge Public Access Site, 272, 275, 282–83
Christenson, P. W., 94
Clark, N. W., 3, 4
Clark Bridge, 170, 171, 177, 186–87
Clark Bridge Road, 175, 177
Coliform bacteria, 17
Compass, 10, 55
Conners Flat Public Access Site, 28, 31, 48–49
Conners Flat Road, 28, 31, 48
County Line Road, 122, 134–35
County Parking Lot (Pigeon River), 122, 123, 126–27
Crawford County, 26, 76
Crocket Bridge, 172, 175, 177, 188–89
Curwood, James Oliver (author, resident of South Branch), 63
Custer (village), 225, 226, 227

Depth of water (for safe wading), 5–7
Devoe Lake, 208, 211, 214, 215
Deward, 95, 97, 98, 102–3
Dissolved oxygen, 15, 17–18
Dobson Bridge Canoe Landing, 255, 266–67
Doc Sehls Bridge, 145, 152–53
Dogtown Public Access Site, 59, 70–71
Dory (boat), 249
Downey, Mr. (former owner of Mason Tract), 53

Downey's Public Access Site, 56, 59, 60, 68–69
Durant, Mr. (builder of the Castle), 53, 67

Earthworks (Indian), 210, 220, 222
East Branch of the Au Sable, 24
East Jordan (town), 272, 273, 275
Edgetts Bridge Public Access Site, 256–57
Edgewater on the Au Sable, 27, 43
Edibility of trout, 11, 15, 16
Electric Weir Public Access Site, 286–87
Ellsworth Road, 273, 275
Elm Flats Canoe Landing, 255, 264–65
Elmira (town), 270
Elmwood Cemetery, 29
Emergence dates (of flies), 12–13
Erosion, 20
Escanaba River, 10

Farming. See Agriculture
Federation of Fly Fishers (FFF), 11, 22
Fisheries biologists, 21
Fish hatchery (Grayling), 29
Fish kill, 19, 120
Fish ladders, 192
Fitzhugh, Daniel, 4
Flashlight, 10
Flies, Michigan trout, 12–13
Flies-only restrictions, 11, 24, 35, 45, 65, 96, 113, 224, 235, 237
Flooding (on Rifle River), 210
Fly-fishing, 2, 24, 35, 43, 52, 76, 85, 103, 105, 131, 142, 170, 192, 208, 224
Fly hatches, 12–13
Flytiers, 12
Forks Bridge (Boardman River), 195, 196
Forks south of Baldwin Public Access Site (Pere Marquette River), 228, 232–33
Forks State Forest Campground (Boardman River), 195, 197, 202–3

Gamble Creek, 208, 209
Gate's Au Sable Lodge, 27, 43
Gaylord (town), 79, 118, 121, 142,
    145, 170, 173, 273
Gaylord Fishing Club, 185
Gibbs Road, 176
Glaciers, 2, 142
Gleason's Landing, 224, 225, 228, 230,
    235, 236–37
Grand Traverse Bay, 192
Graves Crossing State Forest
    Campground, 273, 280–81
Grayling (fish), 3–5, 26, 94
Grayling (town), 17, 24, 28, 29, 59,
    79, 81, 97
Greenbelt zoning, 20
Green Cottage, 226
Green River, 271
Green Timbers Public Access Site,
    144, 146, 148, 157, 158–59
Groundwater, 27, 78, 120, 194, 210
Grousehaven, 215
Grousehaven Lake, 211
Gwinn, 10

Haakwood State Forest Campground,
    143, 144, 147, 149, 164–65
Halladay, Len, 12
Hammonds Bay, 3
Hardwood Lake Road, 123
Hartwick Pines Road, 81
Headquarters Road, 29, 32, 34
Hexagenia limbata, 13, 33, 47, 52, 55
Highbanks (Au Sable River), 39
Highbanks (South Branch Au Sable
    River), 54
High water, 5, 6, 26, 52, 120, 144,
    172, 194, 208, 226
"Holy Water" (Au Sable River), 2,
    24
Houghton Creek, 209
House's Lost Cabin Road, 176
Hydroelectric power dams, 19, 192
Hydrologic setting, 19

Idlewild (village), 224
Impoundments, 19, 120, 192

Indian River (town), 118, 121, 145
Indians, 2, 210
I-75 (highway), 24, 29, 148, 160

Jewett, Harry M., 215
Jordan River, 26, 270–75

Kalkaska (town), 97, 194, 195
Kelloggs Bridge, 80, 81, 92–93
Keystone Landing State Forest
    Campground, 28, 30, 38–39
Kingsley (village), 195
Kinney Creek (Kinne Creek), 227
Kolka Creek Road, 97, 100

Lake Charlevoix, 270, 272
Lake County, 250
Lake Huron, 3, 95
Lake Michigan, 3, 95, 224
Lake St. Helen, 53
Lee, D. B. (former co-owner of Mason
    Tract), 53
Leline Road, 56, 57, 58, 64–65
Limiting the kill, 11, 173
Lincoln Bridge State Forest
    Campground, 255, 262–63
Litter, 20
Little Manistee River, 4
Little South Branch (Pere Marquette
    River), 224, 228, 230, 232–33
Logjams, 9, 120, 144
"Loonsilt," 33
Louie's Landing Road, 28, 30, 36–
    37
Lovejoy, P. S. (Lovejoy Monument),
    123
Lovells (village), 76, 78, 79, 80
Lovells Bridge, 79, 80, 88–89
Lovells Road, 81, 88, 90, 93
Lower Peninsula, 1, 15
Lower Public Access Site (North
    Branch Au Sable River), 79, 80,
    90–91
Ludington, 224, 227
Ludington State Park, 227
Lumbermen, 2, 210
Lupton (village), 211

Luther (town), 254
Luther Highway, 254

McIntosh Landing, 118
Mackenzie River Boats, 249
Mackinac Bridge, 24
McKinnon Bend Public Access Site, 174, 176, 178–79
McMasters Bridge, 25, 31
McMasters Bridge Road, 29, 31
Main River Bridge, 171, 174, 177, 184–85
Mallard Pond, 211
Mancelona (town), 273
Manistee County, 250
Manistee National Forest, 250
Manistee River, 4, 94–117
Manistee River Bridge State Forest Campground, 96, 97, 98, 100, 110–11
Maribou Muddler (fly), 13
Marl, 271, 281, 283
Marquardt Road, 176
Mason, George W., 53, 54
Mason Tract (Mason Grant), 52, 53, 55, 57, 58, 61
Matuka streamer (fly), 13
Mayfield (village), 12
Mershan, A. N., 4
Mershan, William B., 3, 4, 78, 172
M-55 (highway), 254
Michigan Caddis (fly), 12, 13
Michigan Canoe Trails, 9, 193
Michigan Department of Natural Resources (DNR), 15, 17, 20, 21
Michigan Fish Commission, 4
Michigan Fishing Guide, 15
Michigan United Conservation Clubs, 22
Michigan Water Resources Commission, 16
Middle Branch (Pere Marquette River), 226
Military Road, 101, 116
Mt. Bliss Road, 275
M-66 (highway), 273, 275

M-72 (highway and bridge), 29, 30, 31, 96, 97, 98, 99, 100, 110
M-37 (highway), 224, 228, 230, 246, 254
M-37 Bridge south of Baldwin Public Access Site, 224, 228, 230, 234
M-32 (highway), 176
Muddler Minnow (fly), 13

National Guard Artillery Range, 78
National Scenic River, 224
Native trout, 3, 270
Natural River Plan, 192, 210, 224
Night wading, 6
No-kill water, 65, 67, 69
Norris, Thadeus, 94
North Branch Au Sable River, 52, 76–93
North Branch Boardman River, 192, 195, 196, 198, 199
North Branch Bridge (Boardman River), 195, 196, 198–99
North Down River Road, 29, 31, 32
North Sharon Road, 99, 101, 116–17
North Sharon Road Bridge, 99, 101, 116–17
Numbered Roads (Pine River), 251

Ogemaw Center Road, 218
Ogemaw County, 208, 210
Oil and gas development, 121, 173
Oil slicks, 16
Old Bridge Public Access Site, 271
"Old man's fishing," 77
Old State Road, 275
Old U.S. 27 (highway), 81, 97, 145, 149, 162, 166, 168
Old Vanderbilt Road, 122, 123, 128, 146, 148, 154
Old Vanderbilt Road Bridge (Pigeon River), 119, 122, 123, 128–29
Old Vanderbilt Road Bridge (Sturgeon River), 145, 146, 154–55
Onaway, 173, 176
"Ootawas" River, 194
Osmun Road, 124, 125
Otsego County, 76, 124, 170

Otsego Lake, 76
Otsego Lake State Park, 79

Passenger pigeon, 121
Paw Paw River, 4
Pazanier, Rudolf, 194
Pere Marquette Fishing Club, 226
Pere Marquette Railroad, 227
Pere Marquette River, 8, 16, 224–26
Peterson Bridge, 249, 250, 255
Peterson Bridge National Forest
    Campground, 255, 269–70
Peters Road, 212, 213, 218, 220–21
Pigeon Bridge State Forest
    Campground, 119, 121, 122, 130–31
Pigeon River, 3, 19, 96, 118–41, 142
Pigeon River State Forest
    Campground, 122, 123, 132–33
Pigeon River Trout Research Station,
    121
Pine Grove State Forest Campground,
    119, 122, 124, 138–39
Pine River, 246–69
Pinney Bridge Public Access Site, 273,
    278–79
Pioneer Road, 57
Pipe Springs Public Access Site, 78,
    79, 80, 82–83
Pleistocene glaciation, 2, 15, 142
Pollution, 15–16
Pollution Emergency Alerting System,
    16
Poquette Road, 145, 146, 150
Poquette Road Bridge, 145, 146, 150–51
Portaging, 9
Public Health Advisory (contaminated
    fish cautions), 11, 15, 16

Quicksand, 7

Rainbow Bend State Forest
    Campground, 28, 31, 50–51
Rainbow Rapids, 9, 225, 226
Rainbow trout, 3–5, 43, 227
Ranch Road, 211, 214

Ranch Rudolf, 194
Raymond Road, 251
Red Bridge (Manistee River), 98, 100,
    106–7
Red Bridge (Pigeon River), 122, 124,
    125, 140–41
Rifle River, 208–23
Rifle River Recreation Area, 210, 211,
    212, 214–15
Rifle River State Forest Campground,
    212, 213, 218–19
Riverbanks, 19, 39, 67, 107
Riverbed, 19–20
Robert's Yellow Drake (fly), 12
Rogers Road Bridge Public Access
    Site, 275, 289–90
Rondo Road, 147, 149, 166
Rondo Road Bridge Public Access
    Site, 147, 149, 166–67
Roscommon, 17, 53, 54, 55
Rose City, 208, 211, 212, 213
Rose City Road, 211
Round Lake Campground, 173, 176
Round Lake Road, 123
Rule of ten (for wading), 5–6

Safety, 5–11, 23, 144, 172, 225
Sage Lake Road, 208, 209, 212, 213,
    215, 216–17
Salmon, Atlantic and Pacific, 20–21,
    224
Sandy Bottom Public Access Site, 99,
    114–15
Sawdust Pile Road, 176
Scheck's Place State Forest
    Campground, 194, 195, 196, 197,
    206–7
Scott Road, 147, 149
Scott Road Public Access Site, 147,
    148, 149, 162–63
Scottville, 225, 227
Selkirk, 208, 209, 210, 211, 212, 222
Selkirk Bridge, 212, 213, 222–23
Sewage disposal, 17–18
Sharon (village), 96, 97, 99, 101
Sheep Ranch Public Access Site, 76,
    77, 80, 84–85

Shupac Lake State Forest
  Campground, 79, 84, 86
Silver Creek State Forest
  Campground, 255, 260–61
Skookum Bridge, 254, 258–59
Skookum Road, 254, 255
Skunk (fly), 12, 13
Smith Bridge Public Access Site, 53,
  54, 56, 60, 74–75
Song of the Morning Ranch Pond,
  119, 120
South Branch Au Sable River, 7, 17,
  25, 52–75
South Branch Boardman River, 192,
  195, 196, 198, 200, 202
South Branch Bridge (Boardman
  River), 195, 200–201
South Branch Road (Pere Marquette
  River), 229, 230, 231, 240, 242
South Branch Road (South Branch
  Au Sable River), 56, 57, 59, 60
South Down River Road, 29, 30, 34,
  36, 38, 40
South Tower Public Access Site, 174,
  182–83
Sparr Road, 176
Spawning (trout), 15, 19
Special regulations, 11
Spin fishing, 2, 35, 63, 83, 86, 103,
  127, 142, 151, 165, 179, 199
"Spreads" (on Black River), 171
State Road, 254, 255
Steelhead trout, 2, 95, 208, 224
Stephan, Dan, 26
Stephan Bridge Public Access Site, 30,
  42–43
"Stillwater" (Au Sable River), 25, 47,
  49, 51
Sturgeon Bridge, 142, 146, 148, 156–
  57
Sturgeon River, 3, 7, 142–69
Sturgeon Valley Road, 121, 123, 156,
  158
Sulak Public Access Site, 229, 240–
  41
Sunset Trail Road, 100, 112
Sweepers, 9

Temperature, water, 15–16, 27, 53, 55,
  78, 94, 120, 144, 172, 194, 210, 226
Thendara Road, 28, 30, 40–41
Timber Creek Campground, 227
Tin Bridge, 124, 125
Tin Bridge Public Access Site, 124,
  136–37
Tin Shanty Bridge, 170, 171, 173, 174,
  176, 180–81
Tin Shanty Bridge Road, 174, 176
Tippy Dam, 246, 250
Tobacco River, 4
Topographic maps referenced, 10, 12,
  249–50
Tower (village), 177
Tower Pond, 170, 172
Town Corner Lake State Forest
  Campground, 171, 173
Traverse City, 194, 195
Traverse City Fly Club, 194
Traverse City State Park, 195
Trout habitat, preservation of, 15–22
Trout Unlimited (TU), 11, 22
Trout versus salmon, 20–21
Trowbridge Road, 142, 143, 147, 148
Trowbridge Road Public Access Site,
  147, 148, 160–61
Twin Bridge, 79, 80, 84, 86–87
Twin Bridge Road, 79, 80, 82, 84, 86,
  88
Twin Lake Road (Pigeon River), 122,
  123
Twin Lake Road (Rifle River), 212,
  213, 218

Underwater hazards, 6
Upper Branch Bridge Public Access
  Site, 229, 230, 231, 242–43
Upper Manistee River State Forest
  Campground, 96, 97, 98, 108–9
Upper Peninsula, 3, 16–17
U.S. Forest Service, 224, 226, 227, 239
U.S. Geological Survey, 10
U.S. Highway 10, 254

Vanderbilt (village), 118, 121, 145,
  146

Velocity, stream, 1, 5, 24, 25, 52, 77, 143, 144, 194

Wading safety, 5–7
Wading staff, 6
Wakeley Bridge, 24, 25, 26, 28, 44
Wakeley Bridge Public Access Site, 28, 30, 44–45
Wakeley Bridge Road, 28, 30, 31, 44
Walhalla, 225, 229, 230
Walhalla Bridge Public Access Site, 229, 231, 244–245
Walker Bridge, 250
Water pollution, 15–18
Water quality, 15–18
Water Quality Surveillance Section (Water Resources Commission), 16
Webb Road, 124, 125
Webster Bridge Public Access Site, 275, 284–85
Wells, effect of, on streamflow, 18

West Branch (Sturgeon River), 143
West Sharon Road, 101, 116
Wexford County, 250
Whirlpool (on the Au Sable River), 7, 39
Whirlpool Road, 38, 39
Whitefish, 47, 226
White Pine Canoe State Forest Campground, 28, 30, 46–47
White Road, 147, 149
White Road Bridge, 147, 149, 168
Whitmarsh Road, 145, 146, 152
Wigglesworth Road Public Easement, 175, 176, 190–91
Wilkins Creek, 209
Williamsburg, 195, 196
Williamsburg Road, 195, 196
Winnie, Art, 194
Wolverine (village), 118, 121, 143, 145, 147, 148, 149
Wolverine Road, 124, 147
Worm fishing. *See* Bait fishing